THE GREAT GERMAN COMPOSERS

By George T. Ferris

Table of Contents

NOTE. 5
BACH. 5
HANDEL. 9
GLUCK 27
HAYDN. 33
MOZART. 41
BEETHOVEN. 48
SCHUBERT, SCHUMANN, AND FRANZ. 59
CHOPIN. 68
WEBER. 76
MENDELSSOHN. 82
RICHARD WAGNER. 86

NOTE.

The sketches of composers contained in this volume may seem arbitrary in the space allotted to them. The special attention given to certain names has been prompted as much by their association with great art-epochs as by the consideration of their absolute rank as composers.

The introduction of Chopin, born a Pole, and for a large part of his life a resident of France, among the German composers, may require an explanatory word. Chopin's whole early training was in the German school, and he may be looked on as one of the founders of the latest school of pianoforte composition, whose highest development is in contemporary Germany. He represents German music by his affinities and his influences in art, and bears too close a relation to important changes in musical form to be omitted from this series.

The authorities to which the author is most indebted for material are: Schoelcher's "Life of Handel;" Liszt's "Life of Chopin;" Elise Polko's "Reminiscences;" Lampadius's "Life of Mendelssohn;" Chorley's "Reminiscences;" Urbino's "Musical Composers;" Franz Heuffner's "Wagner and the Music of the Future;" Haweis's "Music and Morals;" and articles in the leading Cyclopædias.

BACH.
I.

The growth and development of German music are eminently noteworthy facts in the history of the fine arts. In little more than a century and a half it reached its present high and brilliant place, its progress being so consecutive and regular that the composers who illustrated its well-defined epochs might fairly have linked hands in one connected series.

To Johann Sebastian Bach must be accorded the title of "father of modern music." All succeeding composers have bowed with reverence before his name, and acknowledged in him the creative mind which not only placed music on a deep scientific basis, but perfected the form from which have been developed the wonderfully rich and varied phases of orchestral composition.

Handel, who was his contemporary, having been born the same year, spoke of him with sincere admiration, and called him the giant of music. Haydn wrote: "Whoever understands me knows that I owe much to Sebastian Bach, that I have studied him thoroughly and well, and that I acknowledge him only as my model." Mozart's unceasing research brought to light many of his unpublished manuscripts, and helped Germany to a full appreciation of this great master. In like manner have the other luminaries of music placed on record their sense of obligation to one whose name is obscure to the general public in comparison with many of his brother composers.

Sebastian Bach was born at Eisenach on the 21st of March, 1685, the son of one of the court musicians. Left in the care of his elder brother, who was an organist, his brilliant powers displayed themselves at an early period. He was the descendant of a race of musicians, and even at that date the wide-spread branches of the family held annual gatherings of a musical character. Young Bach mastered for himself, without much assistance, a thorough musical education at Lüne-burg, where he studied in the gymnasium and sang in the cathedral choir; and at the age of eighteen we find him court musician at Weimar, where a few years later he became organist and director of concerts. He had in the mean time studied the organ at Lübeck under the celebrated Buxtehude, and made himself thoroughly a master of the great Italian composers of sacred music—Palestrina, Lotti, Vivaldi, and others.

At this period Germany was beginning to experience its musical *renaissance*. The various German courts felt that throb of life and enthusiasm which had distinguished the Italian principalities in the preceding century in the direction of painting and sculpture. Every little capital was a focus of artistic rays, and there was a general spirit of rivalry among the princes, who aspired to cultivate the arts of peace as well as those of war. Bach had become known as a gifted musician, not only by his wonderful powers as an organist, but by two of his earlier masterpieces—"Gott ist mein König" and "Ich hatte viel Bektlmmerniss." Under the influence of an atmosphere so artistic, Bach's ardor for study increased with his success, and his rapid advancement in musical power met with warm appreciation.

While Bach held the position of director of the chapel of Prince Leopold of Anhalt-Kothen, which he assumed about the year 1720, he went to Hamburg on a pilgrimage to see old Reinke, then nearly a centenarian, whose fame as an organist was national, and had long been the object of Bach's enthusiasm. The aged man listened while his youthful rival improvised on the old choral, "Upon the Rivers of Babylon." He shed tears of joy while he tenderly embraced Bach, and said: "I did think that this art would die with me; but I see that you will keep it alive."

Our musician rapidly became known far and wide throughout the musical centres of Germany as a learned and recondite composer, as a brilliant improviser, and as an organist beyond rivalry. Yet it was in these last two capacities that his reputation among his contemporaries was the most marked. It was left to a succeeding generation to fully enlighten the world in regard to his creative powers as a musical thinker.

II.

Though Bach's life was mostly spent at Weimar and Leipsic, he was at successive periods chapel-master and concert-director at several of the German courts, which aspired to shape public taste in matters of musical culture and enthusiasm. But he was by nature singularly retiring and unobtrusive, and he recoiled from several brilliant offers which would have brought him too much in contact with the gay world of fashion, apparently dreading any diversion from a severe and exclusive art-life; for within these limits all his hopes, energies, and wishes were focalized. Yet he was not without that keen spirit of rivalry, that love of combat, which seems to be native to spirits of the more robust and energetic type.

In the days of the old Minnesingers, tournaments of music shared the public taste with tournaments of arms. In Bach's time these public competitions were still in vogue. One of these was held by Augustus II., Elector of Saxony and King of Poland, one of the most munificent art-patrons of Europe, but best known to fame from his intimate part in the wars of Charles XII. of Sweden and Peter the Great of Russia. Here Bach's principal rival was a French *virtuoso*, Marchand, who, an exile from Paris, had delighted the king by the lightness and brilliancy of his execution. They were both to improvise on the same theme. Marchand heard Bach's performance, and signalized his own inferiority by declining to play, and secretly leaving the city of Dresden. Augustus sent Bach a hundred louis d'or, but this splendid *douceur* never reached him, as it was appropriated by one of the court officials.

In Bach's half-century of a studious musical life there is but little of stirring incident to record. The significance of his career was interior, not exterior. Twice married, and the father of twenty children, his income was always small even for that age. Yet, by frugality, the simple wants of himself and his family never overstepped the limit of supply; for he seems to have been happily mated with wives who sympathized with his exclusive devotion to art, and united with this the virtues of old-fashioned German thrift.

Three years before his death, Bach, who had a son in the service of the King of Prussia, yielded to the urgent invitation of that monarch to go to Berlin. Frederick II., the conqueror of Rossbach, and one of the greatest of modern soldiers, was a passionate lover of literature and art, and it was his pride to collect at his court all the leading lights of European culture. He was not only the patron of Voltaire, whose connection with the Prussian monarch has furnished such rich material to the anecdote-history of literature, but of all the distinguished painters, poets, and musicians, whom he could persuade by his munificent offers (but rarely fulfilled) to suffer the burden of his eccentricities. Frederick was not content with playing the part of patron, but must himself also be poet, philosopher, painter, and composer.

On the night of Bach's arrival Frederick was taking part in a concert at his palace, and, on hearing that the great musician whose name was in the mouths of all Germany had come, immediately sent for him without allowing him to don a court dress, interrupting his concert with the enthusiastic announcement, "Gentlemen, Bach is here." The cordial hospitality and admiration of Frederick was gratefully acknowledged by Bach, who dedicated to him a three-part fugue on a theme composed by the king, known under the name of "A Musical Offering." But he could not be persuaded to remain long from his Leipsic home.

Shortly before Bach's death, he was seized with blindness, brought on by incessant labor; and his end was supposed to have been hastened by the severe inflammation consequent on two operations performed by an English oculist. He departed this life July 30, 1750, and was buried in St. John's churchyard, universally mourned by musical Germany, though his real title to exceptional greatness was not to be read until the next generation.

III.

Sebastian Bach was not only the descendant of a widely-known musical family, but was himself the direct ancestor of about sixty of the best-known organists and church composers of Germany. As a master of organ-playing, tradition tells us that no one has been his equal, with the possible exception of Handel. He was also an able performer on various stringed instruments, and his preference for the clavichord * led him to write a method for that instrument, which has been the basis of all succeeding methods for the piano. Bach's teachings and influence may be said to have educated a large number of excellent composers and organ and piano players, among whom were Emanuel Bach, Cramer, Hummel, and Clementi; and on his school of theory and practice the best results in music have been built.

* An old instrument which may be called the nearest
prototype of the modern square piano.

That Bach's glory as a composer should be largely posthumous is probably the result of his exceeding simplicity and diffidence, for he always shrank from popular applause; therefore we may believe his compositions were not placed in the proper light during his life. It was through Mozart, Haydn, and Beethoven, that the musical world learned what a master-spirit had wrought in the person of John Sebastian Bach. The first time Mozart heard one of Bach's hymns, he said, "Thank God! I learn something absolutely new." Bach's great compositions include his "Preludes and Fugues" for the organ, works so difficult and elaborate as perhaps to be above the average comprehension, but sources of delight and instruction to all musicians; the "Matthäus Passion," for two choruses and two orchestras, one of the masterpieces in music, which was not produced till a century after it was written; the "Oratorio of the Nativity of Jesus Christ;" and a very large number of masses, anthems, cantatas, chorals, hymns, etc. These works, from their largeness and dignity of form, as also from their depth of musical science, have been to all succeeding composers an art-armory, whence they have derived and furbished their brightest weapons. In the study of Bach's works the student finds the deepest and highest reaches in the science of music; for his mind seems to have grasped all its resources, and to have embodied them with austere purity and precision of form. As Spenser is called the poet for poets, and Laplace the mathematician for mathematicians, so Bach is the musician for musicians. While Handel may be considered a purely independent and parallel growth, it is not too much to assert that without Sebastian Bach and his matchless studies for the piano, organ, and orchestra, we could not have had the varied musical development in sonata and symphony from such masters as Haydn, Mozart, and Beethoven. Three of Sebastian Bach's sons became distinguished musicians, and to Emanuel we owe the artistic development of the sonata, which in its turn became the foundation of the symphony.

HANDEL.

I.

To the modern Englishman Handel is almost a contemporary. Paintings and busts of this great minstrel are scattered everywhere throughout the land. He lies in Westminster Abbey among the great poets, warriors, and statesmen, a giant memory in his noble art. A few hours after death the sculptor Roubiliac took a cast of his face, which he wrought into imperishable marble; "moulded in colossal calm," he towers above his tomb, and accepts the homage of the world benignly like a god. Exeter Hall and the Foundling Hospital in London are also adorned with marble statues of him.

There are more than fifty known pictures of Handel, some of them by distinguished artists. In the best of these pictures Handel is seated in the gay costume of the period, with sword, shot-silk breeches, and coat embroidered with gold. The face is noble in its repose. Benevolence is seated about the finely-shaped mouth, and the face wears the mellow dignity of years, without weakness or austerity. There are few collectors of prints in England and America who have not a woodcut or a lithograph of him. His face and his music are alike familiar to the English-speaking world.

Handel came to England in the year 1710, at the age of twenty-five. Four years before he had met, at Naples, Scarlatti, Porpora, and Corelli. That year had been the turning-point in his life. With one stride he reached the front rank, and felt that no musician alive could teach him anything.

George Frederick Handel (or Händel, as the name is written in German) was born at Halle, Lower Saxony, in the year 1685. Like German literature, German music is a comparatively recent growth. What little feeling existed for the musical art employed itself in cultivating the alien flowers of Italian song. Even eighty years after this Mozart and Haydn were treated like lackeys and vagabonds, just as great actors were treated in England at the same period. Handel's father looked on music as an occupation having very little dignity.

Determined that his young son should become a doctor like himself, and leave the divine art to Italian fiddlers and French buffoons, he did not allow him to go to a public school even, for fear he should learn the gamut. But the boy Handel, passionately fond of sweet sounds, had, with the connivance of his nurse, hidden in the garret a poor spinet, and in stolen hours taught himself how to play. At last the senior Handel had a visit to make to another son in the service of the Duke of Saxe-Weissenfels, and the young George was taken along to the ducal palace. The boy strayed into the chapel, and was irresistibly drawn to the organ. His stolen performance was made known to his father and the duke, and the former was very much enraged at such a direct evidence of disobedience. The duke, however, being astonished at the performance of the youthful genius, interceded for him, and recommended that his taste should be encouraged and cultivated instead of repressed.

From this time forward fortune showered upon him a combination of conditions highly favorable to rapid development. Severe training, ardent friendship, the society of the first composers, and incessant practice were vouchsafed him. As the pupil of the great organist Zachau, he studied the whole existing mass of German and Italian music, and soon exacted from his master the admission that he had nothing more to teach him. Thence he went to Berlin to study the opera-school, where Ariosti and Bononcini were favorite composers. The first was friendly, but the latter, who with a first-rate head had a cankered heart, determined to take the conceit out of the Saxon boy. He challenged him to play at sight an elaborate piece. Handel played it with perfect precision, and thenceforward Bononcini, though he hated the youth as a rival, treated him as an equal.

On the death of his father Handel secured an engagement at the Hamburg opera-house, where he soon made his mark by the ability with which, on several occasions, he conducted rehearsals.

At the age of nineteen Handel received the offer of the Lübeck organ, on condition that he would marry the daughter of the retiring organist. He went down with his friend Mattheson, who it seems had been offered the same terms. They both returned, however, in single blessedness to Hamburg.

Though the Lübeck maiden had stirred no bad blood between them, musical rivalry did. A dispute in the theatre resulted in a duel. The only thing that saved Handel's life was a great brass button that shivered his antagonist's point, when they were parted to become firm friends again.

While at Hamburg Handel's first two operas were composed, "Almira" and "Nero." Both of these were founded on dark tales of crime and sorrow, and, in spite of some beautiful airs and clever instrumentation, were musical failures, as might be expected.

Handel had had enough of manufacturing operas in Germany, and so in July, 1706, he went to Florence. Here he was cordially received; for Florence was second to no city in Italy in its passion for encouraging the arts. Its noble specimens of art creations in architecture, painting, and sculpture, produced a powerful impression upon the young musician. In little more than a week's time he composed an opera, "Rodrigo," for which he obtained one hundred sequins. His next visit was to Venice, where he arrived at the height of the carnival. Whatever effect Venice, with its weird and mysterious beauty, with its marble palaces, façades, pillars, and domes, its magnificent shrines and frescoes, produced on Handel, he took Venice by storm. Handel's power as an organist and a harpsichord player was only second to his strength as a composer, even when, in the full zenith of his maturity, he composed the "Messiah" and "Judas Maccabæus."

"Il caro Sassone," the dear Saxon, found a formidable opponent as well as dear friend in the person of Scarlatti. One night at a masked ball, given by a nobleman, Handel was present in disguise. He sat at the harpsichord, and astonished the company with his playing; but no one could tell who it was that ravished the ears of the assembly. Presently another masquerader came into the room, walked up to the instrument, and called out: "It is either the devil or the Saxon!" This was Scarlatti, who afterward had with Handel, in Florence and Rome, friendly contests of skill, in which it seemed difficult to decide which was victor. To satisfy the Venetian public, Handel composed the opera "Agrippina," which made a *furore* among all the connoisseurs of the city.

So, having seen the summer in Florence and the carnival in Venice, he must hurry on to be in time for the great Easter celebrations in Rome. Here he lived under the patronage of Cardinal Otto-boni, one of the wealthiest and most liberal of the Sacred College. The cardinal was a modern representative of the ancient patrician. Living himself in princely luxury, he endowed hospitals and surgeries for the public. He distributed alms, patronized men of science and art, and entertained the public with comedies, operas, oratorios, puppet-shows, and academic disputes. Under the auspices of this patron, Handel composed three operas and two oratorios. Even at this early period the young composer was parting company with the strict old musical traditions, and his works showed an extraordinary variety and strength of treatment.

From Rome he went to Naples, where he spent his second Italian summer, and composed the original Italian "Aci e Galatea," which in its English version, afterward written for the Duke of Chandos, has continued a marked favorite with the musical world. Thence, after a lingering return through the sunny land where he had been so warmly welcomed, and which had taught him most effectually, in convincing him that his musical life had nothing in common with the traditions of Italian musical art, he returned to Germany, settling at the court of George of Brunswick, Elector of Hanover, and afterward King of England. He received commission in the course of a few months from the elector to visit England, having been warmly invited thither by some English noblemen. On his return to Hanover, at the end of six months, he found the dull and pompous little court unspeakably tiresome after the bustle of London. So it is not to be marveled at that he took the earliest opportunity of returning to the land which he afterward adopted. At this period he was not yet twenty-five years old, but already famous as a performer on the organ and harpsichord, and as a composer of Italian operas.

When Queen Anne died and Handel's old patron became King of England, Handel was forbidden to appear before him, as he had not forgotten the musician's escapade; but his peace was at last made by a little ruse. Handel had a friend at court, Baron Kilmansegge, from whom he learned that the king was, on a certain day, going to take an excursion on the Thames. So he set to work to compose music for the occasion, which he arranged to have performed on a boat which followed the king's barge. As the king floated down the river he heard the new and delightful "Water-Music." He knew that only one man could have composed such music; so he sent for Handel, and sealed his pardon with a pension of two hundred pounds a year.

II.

Let us take a glance at the society in which the composer moved in the heyday of his youth. His greatness was to be perfected in after-years by bitter rivalries, persecution, alternate oscillations of poverty and affluence, and a multitude of bitter experiences. But at this time Handel's life was a serene and delightful one. Rival factions had not been organized to crush him. Lord Burlington lived much at his mansion, which was then out of town, although the house is now in the heart of Piccadilly. The intimate friendship of this nobleman helped to bring the young musician into contact with many distinguished people.

It is odd to think of the people Handel met daily without knowing that their names and his would be in a century famous. The following picture sketches Handel and his friends in a sprightly fashion:

"Yonder heavy, ragged-looking youth standing at the corner of Regent Street, with a slight and rather more refined-looking companion, is the obscure Samuel Johnson, quite unknown to fame. He is walking with Richard Savage. As Signor Handel, 'the composer of Italian music,' passes by, Savage becomes excited, and nudges his friend, who takes only a languid interest in the foreigner. Johnson did not care for music; of many noises he considered it the least disagreeable.

"Toward Charing Cross comes, in shovel-hat and cassock, the renowned ecclesiastic Dean Swift. He has just nodded patronizingly to Bononcini in the Strand, and suddenly meets Handel, who cuts him dead. Nothing disconcerted, the dean moves on, muttering his famous epigram:

'Some say that Signor Bononcini,
Compared to Handel, is a ninny;
While others vow that to him Handel
Is hardly fit to hold a candle.
Strange that such difference should be
'Twixt tweedledum and tweedledee.'

"As Handel enters the 'Turk's Head' at the corner of Regent Street, a noble coach and four drives up. It is the Duke of Chandos, who is inquiring for Mr. Pope. Presently a deformed little man, in an iron-gray suit, and with a face as keen as a razor, hobbles out, makes a low bow to the burly Handel, who, helping him into the chariot, gets in after him, and they drive off together to Cannons, the duke's mansion at Edge-ware. There they meet Mr. Addison, the poet Gay, and the witty Arbuthnot, who have been asked to luncheon. The last number of the *Spectator* is on the table, and a brisk discussion soon arises between Pope and Addison concerning the merits of the Italian opera, in which Pope would have the better if he only knew a little more about music, and could keep his temper. Arbuthnot sides with Pope in favor of Mr. Handel's operas; the duke endeavors to keep the peace. Handel probably uses his favorite exclamation, 'Vat te tevil I care!' and consumes the *recherche* wines and rare viands with undiminished gusto.

"The Magnificent, or the Grand Duke, as he was called, had built himself a palace for £230,000. He had a private chapel, and appointed Handel organist in the room of the celebrated Dr. Pepusch, who retired with excellent grace before one manifestly his superior. On week-days the duke and duchess entertained all the wits and grandees in town, and on Sundays the Edgeware Road was thronged with the gay equipages of those who went to worship at the ducal chapel and hear Mr. Handel play on the organ.

"The Edgeware Road was a pleasant country drive, but parts of it were so solitary that highwaymen were much to be feared. The duke was himself attacked on one occasion; and those who could afford it never traveled so far out of town without armed retainers. Cannons was the pride of the neighborhood, and the duke—of whom Pope wrote,

'Thus gracious Chandos is beloved at sight'—

was as popular as he was wealthy. But his name is made still more illustrious by the Chandos anthems. They were all written at Cannons between 1718 and 1720, and number in all eleven overtures, thirty-two solos, six duets, a trio, quartet, and forty-seven choruses. Some of the above are real masterpieces; but, with the exception of 'The waves of the sea rage horribly,' and 'Who is God but the Lord?' few of them are ever heard now. And yet these anthems were most significant in the variety of the choruses and in the range of the accompaniments; and it was then, no doubt, that Handel was feeling his way toward the great and immortal sphere of his oratorio music. Indeed, his first oratorio, 'Esther,' was composed at Cannons, as also the English version of 'Acis and Galatea.'"

But Handel had other associates, and we must now visit Thomas Britton, the musical coal-heaver. "There goes the famous small-coal man, a lover of learning, a musician, and a companion of gentlemen." So the folks used to say as Thomas Britton, the coal-heaver of Clerkenwell Green, paced up and down the neighboring streets with his sack of small coal on his back, destined for one of his customers. Britton was great among the great. He was courted by the most fashionable folk of his day. He was a cultivated coal-heaver, who, besides his musical taste and ability, possessed an extensive knowledge of chemistry and the occult sciences.

Britton did more than this. He gave concerts in Aylesbury Street, Clerkenwell, where this singular man had formed a dwelling-house, with a concert-room and a coal-store, out of what was originally a stable. On the ground-floor was the small-coal repository, and over that the concert-room—very long and narrow, badly lighted, and with a ceiling so low that a tall man could scarcely stand upright in it. The stairs to this room were far from pleasant to ascend, and the following facetious lines by Ward, the author of the "London Spy," confirm this:

"Upon Thursdays repair
To my palace, and there
Hobble up stair by stair
But I pray ye take care
That you break not your shins by a stumble;

"And without e'er a souse
Paid to me or my spouse,
Sit as still as a mouse

At the top of the house,
And there you shall hear how we fumble."

Nevertheless beautiful duchesses and the best society in town flocked to Britton's on Thursdays—not to order coals, but to sit out his concerts.

Let us follow the short, stout little man on a concert-day. The customers are all served, or as many as can be. The coal-shed is made tidy and swept up, and the coal-heaver awaits his company. There he stands at the door of his stable, dressed in his blue blouse, dustman's hat, and maroon kerchief tightly fastened round his neck. The concert-room is almost full, and, pipe in hand, Britton awaits a new visitor—the beautiful Duchess of B———. She is somewhat late (the coachman, possibly, is not quite at home in the neighborhood).

Here comes a carriage, which stops at the coal-shop; and, laying down his pipe, the coal-heaver assists her grace to alight, and in the genteelest manner escorts her to the narrow staircase leading to the music-room. Forgetting Ward's advice, she trips laughingly and carelessly up the stairs to the room, from which proceed faint sounds of music, increasing to quite an *olla podri-da* of sound as the apartment is reached—for the musicians are tuning up. The beautiful duchess is soon recognized, and as soon in deep gossip with her friends. But who is that gentlemanly man leaning over the chamber-organ? That is Sir Roger L'Estrange, an admirable performer on the violoncello, and a great lover of music. He is watching the subtile fingering of Mr. Handel, as his dimpled hands drift leisurely and marvelously over the keys of the instrument.

There, too, is Mr. Bannister with his fiddle—the first Englishman, by-the-by, who distinguished himself upon the violin; there is Mr. Woolaston, the painter, relating to Dr. Pepusch of how he had that morning thrown up his window upon hearing Britton crying "Small coal!" near his house in Warwick Lane, and, having beckoned him in, had made a sketch for a painting of him; there, too, is Mr. John Hughes, author of the "Siege of Damascus." In the background also are Mr. Philip Hart, Mr. Henry Symonds, Mr. Obadiah Shuttleworth, Mr. Abiell Whichello; while in the extreme corner of the room is Robe, a justice of the peace, letting out to Henry Needier of the Excise Office the last bit of scandal that has come into his court. And now, just as the concert has commenced, in creeps "Soliman the Magnificent," also known as Mr. Charles Jennens, of Great Ormond Street, who wrote many of Handel's librettos, and arranged the words for the "Messiah."

"Soliman the Magnificent" is evidently resolved to do justice to his title on this occasion with his carefully-powdered wig, frills, maroon-colored coat, and buckled shoes; and as he makes his progress up the room, the company draw aside for him to reach his favorite seat near Handel. A trio of Corelli's is gone through; then Madame Cuzzoni sings Handel's last new air; Dr. Pepusch takes his turn at the harpsichord; another trio of Hasse, or a solo on the violin by Bannister; a selection on the organ from Mr. Handel's new oratorio; and then the day's programme is over.

Dukes, duchesses, wits and philosophers, poets and musicians, make their way down the satirized stairs to go, some in carriages, some in chairs, some on foot, to their own palaces, houses, or lodgings.

III.

We do not now think of Handel in connection with the opera. To the modern mind he is so linked to the oratorio, of which he was the father and the consummate master, that his operas are curiosities but little known except to musical antiquaries. Yet some of the airs from the Handel operas are still cherished by singers as among the most beautiful songs known to the concert-stage.

In 1720 Handel was engaged by a party of noblemen, headed by his Grace of Chandos, to compose operas for the Royal Academy of Music at the Haymarket. An attempt had been made to put this institution on a firm foundation by a subscription of £50,000, and it was opened on May 2d with a full company of singers engaged by Handel. In the course of eight years twelve operas were produced in rapid succession: "Floridante," December 9, 1721; "Ottone," January 12, 1723; "Flavio" and "Giulio Cesare," 1723; "Tamerlano," 1724; "Rodelinda," 1725; "Scipione," 1726; "Alessandro," 1726; "Admeto," 727; "Siroe," 1728; and "Tolommeo," 1728. They made as great a *furore* among the musical public of that day as would an opera from Gounod or Verdi in the present. The principal airs were sung throughout the land, and published as harpsichord pieces; for in these halcyon days of our composers the whole atmosphere of the land was full of the flavor and color of Handel. Many of the melodies in these now forgotten operas have been worked up by modern composers, and so have passed into modern music unrecognized. It is a notorious fact that the celebrated song, "Where the Bee sucks," by Dr. Arne, is taken from a movement in "Rinaldo." Thus the new life of music is ever growing rich with the dead leaves of the past. The most celebrated of these operas was entitled "Otto." It was a work composed of one long string of exquisite gems, like Mozart's "Don Giovanni" and Gounod's "Faust." Dr. Pepusch, who had never quite forgiven Handel for superseding him as the best organist in England, remarked, of one of the airs, "That great bear must have been inspired when he wrote that air." The celebrated Madame Cuzzoni made her *début* in it. On the second night the tickets rose to four guineas each, and Cuzzoni received two thousand pounds for the season.

The composer had already begun to be known for his irascible temper. It is refreshing to learn that operatic singers of the day, however whimsical and self-willed, were obliged to bend to the imperious genius of this man. In a spirit of ill-timed revolt Cuzzoni declined to sing an air. She had already given him trouble by her insolence and freaks, which at times were unbearable. Handel at last exploded. He flew at the wretched woman and shook her like a rat. "Ah! I always knew you were a fery tevil," he cried, "and I shall now let you know that I am Beelzebub, the prince of de tevils!" and, dragging her to the open window, was just on the point of pitching her into the street when, in every sense of the word, she recanted. So, when Carestini, the celebrated tenor, sent back an air, Handel was furious. Rushing into the trembling Italian's house, he said, in his four- or five-language style: "You tog! don't I know better as yourself vaat it pest for you to sing? If you vill not sing all de song vaat I give you, I vill not pay you ein stiver." Among the anecdotes told of Handel's passion is one growing out of the composer's peculiar sensitiveness to discords. The dissonance of the tuning-up period of an orchestra is disagreeable to the most patient. Handel, being peculiarly sensitive to this unfortunate necessity, always arranged that it should take place before the audience assembled, so as to prevent any sound of scraping or blowing. Unfortunately, on one occasion, some wag got access to the orchestra where the ready-tuned instruments were lying, and with diabolical dexterity put every string and crook out of tune. Handel enters. All the bows are raised together, and at the given beat all start off *con spirito*. The effect was startling in the extreme. The unhappy *maestro* rushes madly from his place, kicks to pieces the first double-bass he sees, and, seizing a kettle-drum, throws it violently at the leader of the band. The effort sends his wig flying, and, rushing bareheaded to the footlights, he stands a few moments amid the roars of the house, snorting with rage and choking with passion. Like Burleigh's nod, Handel's wig seemed to have been a sure guide to his temper. When things went well, it had a certain complacent vibration; but when he was out of humor, the wig indicated the fact in a very positive way. The Princess of Wales was wont to blame her ladies for talking instead of listening. "Hush, hush!" she would say. "Don't you see Handel's wig?"

For several years after the subscription of the nobility had been exhausted, our composer, having invested £10,000 of his own in the Haymarket, produced operas with remarkable affluence, some of them *pasticcio* works, composed of all sorts of airs, in which the singers could give their *bravura songs*. These were "Lotario," 1729; "Partenope," 1730; "Poro," 1731; "Ezio," 1732; "Sosarme," 1732; "Orlando," 1733; "Ariadne," 1734; and also several minor works. Handel's operatic career was not so much the outcome of his choice as dictated to him by the necessity of time and circumstance. As time went on, his operas lost public interest. The audiences dwindled, and the overflowing houses of his earlier experience were replaced by empty benches. This, however, made little difference with Handel's royal patrons. The king and the Prince of Wales, with their respective households, made it an express point to show their deep interest in Handel's success. In illustration of this, an amusing anecdote is told of the Earl of Chesterfield. During the performance of "Rinaldo" this nobleman, then an equerry of the king, was met quietly retiring from the theatre in the middle of the first act. Surprise being expressed by a gentleman who met the earl, the latter said: "I don't wish to disturb his Majesty's privacy."

Handel paid his singers in those days what were regarded as enormous prices. Senisino and Carestini had each twelve hundred pounds, and Cuzzoni two thousand, for the season. Toward the end of what may be called the Handel season nearly all the singers and nobles forsook him, and supported Farinelli, the greatest singer living, at the rival house in Lincoln's Inn Fields.

IV.

From the year 1729 the career of Handel was to be a protracted battle, in which he was sometimes victorious, sometimes defeated, but always undaunted and animated with a lofty sense of his own superior power. Let us take a view of some of the rival musicians with whom he came in contact. Of all these Bononcini was the most formidable. He came to England in 1720 with Ariosti, also a meritorious composer. Factions soon began to form themselves around Handel and Bononcini, and a bitter struggle ensued between these old foes. The same drama repeated itself, with new actors, about thirty years afterward, in Paris. Gluck was then the German hero, supported by Marie Antoinette, and Piccini fought for the Italian opera under the colors of the king's mistress Du Barry, while all the *litterateurs* and nobles ranged themselves on either side in bitter contest. The battle between Handel and Bononcini, as the exponents of German and Italian music, was also repeated in after-years between Mozart and Salieri, Weber and Rossini, and to-day is seen in the acrimonious disputes going on between Wagner and the Italian school. Bononcini's career in England came to an end very suddenly. It was discovered that a madrigal brought out by him was pirated from another Italian composer; whereupon Bononcini left England, humiliated to the dust, and finally died obscure and alone, the victim of a charlatan alchemist, who succeeded in obtaining all his savings.

Another powerful rival of Handel was Porpora, or, as Handel used to call him, "old Borbora." Without Bononcini's fire or Handel's daring originality, he represented the dry contrapuntal school of Italian music. He was also a great singing-master, famous throughout Europe, and upon this his reputation had hitherto principally rested. He came to London in 1733, under the patronage of the Italian faction, especially to serve as a thorn in the side of Handel. His first opera, "Ariadne," was a great success; but when he had the audacity to challenge the great German in the field of oratorio, his defeat was so overwhelming that he candidly admitted his rival's superiority. But he believed that no operas in the world were equal to his own, and he composed fifty of them during his life, extending to the days of Haydn, whom he had the honor of teaching, while the father of the symphony, on the other hand, cleaned Por-pora's boots and powdered his wig for him.

Another Italian opponent was Hasse, a man of true genius, who in his old age instructed some of the most splendid singers in the history of the lyric stage. He also married one of the most gifted and most beautiful divas of Europe, Faustina Bordoni. The following anecdote does equal credit to Hasse's heart and penetration: In after-years, when he had left England, he was again sent for to take Handel's place as conductor of opera and oratorio. Hasse inquired, "What! is Handel dead?" On being told no, he indignantly refused, saying he was not worthy to tie Handel's shoe-latchets.

There are also Dr. Pepusch, the Anglicized Prussian, and Dr. Greene, both names well known in English music. Pepusch had had the leading place, before Handel's arrival, as organist and conductor, and made a distinct place for himself even after the sun of Handel had obscured all of his contemporaries. He wrote the music of the "Beggar's Opera," which was the great sensation of the times, and which still keeps possession of the stage. Pepusch was chiefly notable for his skill in arranging the popular songs of the day, and probably did more than any other composer to give the English ballad its artistic form.

The name of Dr. Greene is best known in connection with choral compositions. His relations with Handel and Bononcini are hardly creditable to him. He seems to have flattered each in turn. He upheld Bononcini in the great madrigal controversy, and appears to have wearied Handel by his repeated visits. The great Saxon easily saw through the flatteries of a man who was in reality an ambitious rival, and joked about him, not always in the best taste. When he was told that Greene was giving concerts at the "Devil Tavern," near Temple Bar, "Ah!" he exclaimed, "mein poor friend Toctor Greene—so he is gone to de Tevil!"

From 1732 to 1740 Handel's life presents the suggestive and often-repeated experience in the lives of men of genius—a soul with a great creative mission, of which it is half unconscious, partly yielding to and partly struggling against the tendencies of the age, yet gradually crystallizing into its true form, and getting consecrated to its true work. In these eight years Handel presented to the public ten operas and five oratorios. It was in 1731 that the great significant fact, though unrecognized by himself and others, occurred, which stamped the true bent of his genius. This was the production of his first oratorio in England. He was already playing his operas to empty houses, the subject of incessant scandal and abuse on the part of his enemies, but holding his way with steady cheerfulness and courage. Twelve years before this he had composed the oratorio of "Esther," but it was still in manuscript, uncared for and neglected. It was finally produced by a society called Philharmonic, under the direction of Bernard Gates, the royal chapel-master. Its fame spread wide, and we read these significant words in one of the old English newspapers: "'Esther,' an English oratorio, was performed six times, and very full."

Shortly after this Handel himself conducted "Esther" at the Haymarket by royal command. His success encouraged him to write "Deborah," another attempt in the same field, and it met a warm reception from the public, March 17, 1733.

For about fifteen years Handel had struggled heroically in the composition of Italian operas. With these he had at first succeeded; but his popularity waned more and more, and he became finally the continued target for satire, scorn, and malevolence. In obedience to the drift of opinion, all the great singers, who had supported him at the outset, joined the rival ranks or left England. In fact it may be almost said that the English public were becoming dissatisfied with the whole system and method of Italian music. Colley Cibber, the actor and dramatist, explains why Italian opera could never satisfy the requirement of Handel, or be anything more than an artificial luxury in England: "The truth is, this kind of entertainment is entirely sensational." Still both Handel and his friends and his foes, all the exponents of musical opinion in England, persevered obstinately in warming this foreign exotic into a new lease of life.

The quarrel between the great Saxon composer and his opponents raged incessantly both in public and private. The newspaper and the drawing-room rang alike with venomous diatribes. Handel was called a swindler, a drunkard, and a blasphemer, to whom Scripture even was not sacred. The idea of setting Holy Writ to music scandalized the Pharisees, who reveled in the licentious operas and love-songs of the Italian school. All the small wits of the time showered on Handel epigram and satire unceasingly. The greatest of all the wits, however, Alexander Pope, was his firm friend and admirer; and in the "Dunciad," wherein the wittiest of poets impaled so many of the small fry of the age with his pungent and vindictive shaft, he also slew some of the most malevolent of Handel's foes.

Fielding, in "Tom Jones," has an amusing hit at the taste of the period: "It was Mr. Western's custom every afternoon, as soon as he was drunk, to hear his daughter play on the harpsichord; for he was a great lover of music, and perhaps, had he lived in town, might have passed as a connoisseur, for he always excepted against the finest compositions of Mr. Handel."

So much had it become the fashion to criticise Handel's new effects in vocal and instrumental composition, that some years later Mr. Sheridan makes one of his characters fire a pistol simply to shock the audience, and makes him say in a stage whisper to the gallery, "This hint, gentlemen, I took from Handel."

The composer's Oxford experience was rather amusing and suggestive. We find it recorded that in July, 1733, "one Handell, a foreigner, was desired to come to Oxford to perform in music." Again the same writer says: "Handell with his lousy crew, a great number of foreign fiddlers, had a performance for his own benefit at the theatre." One of the dons writes of the performance as follows: "This is an innovation; but every one paid his five shillings to try how a little fiddling would sit upon him. And, notwithstanding the barbarous and inhuman combination of such a parcel of unconscionable scamps, he [Handel] disposed of the most of his tickets."

"Handel and his lousy crew," however, left Oxford with the prestige of a magnificent victory. His third oratorio, "Athaliah," was received with vast applause by a great audience. Some of his university admirers, who appreciated academic honors more than the musician did, urged him to accept the degree of Doctor of Music, for which he would have to pay a small fee. The characteristic reply was a Parthian arrow: "Vat te tevil I trow my money away for dat vich the blockhead vish'? I no vant!"

V.

In 1738 Handel was obliged to close the theatre and suspend payment. He had made and spent during his operatic career the sum of £10,000 sterling, besides dissipating the sum of £50,000 subscribed by his noble patrons. The rival house lasted but a few months longer, and the Duchess of Marlborough and her friends, who ruled the opposition clique and imported Bononcini, paid £12,000 for the pleasure of ruining Handel. His failure as an operatic composer is due in part to the same causes which constituted his success in oratorio and cantata. It is a little significant to notice that, alike by the progress of his own genius and by the force of conditions, he was forced out of the operatic field at the very time when he strove to tighten his grip on it.

His free introduction of choral and instrumental music, his creation of new forms and remodeling of old ones, his entire subordination of the words in the story to a pure musical purpose, offended the singers and retarded the action of the drama in the eyes of the audience; yet it was by virtue of these unpopular characteristics that the public mind was being moulded to understand and love the form of the oratorio.

From 1734 to 1738 Handel composed and produced a number of operatic works, the principal ones of which were "Alcina," 1735; "Arminio," 1737; and "Berenice," 1737. He also during these years wrote the magnificent music to Dryden's "Alexander's Feast," and the great funeral anthem on the occasion of Queen Caroline's death in the latter part of the year 1737.

We can hardly solve the tenacity of purpose with which Handel persevered in the composition of operatic music after it had ruined him; but it was still some time before he fully appreciated the true turn of his genius, which could not be trifled with or ignored. In his adversity he had some consolation. His creditors were patient, believing in his integrity. The royal family were his firm friends.

Southey tells us that Handel, having asked the youthful Prince of Wales, then a child, and afterward George the Third, if he loved music, answered, when the prince expressed his pleasure: "A good boy, a good boy! You shall protect my fame when I am dead." Afterward, when the half-imbecile George was crazed with family and public misfortunes, he found his chief solace in the Waverley novels and Handel's music.

It is also an interesting fact that the poets and thinkers of the age were Handel's firm admirers. Such men as Gay, Arbuthnot, Hughes, Colley Cibber, Pope, Fielding, Hogarth, and Smollett, who recognized the deep, struggling tendencies of the times, measured Handel truly. They defended him in print, and never failed to attend his performances, and at his benefit concerts their enthusiastic support always insured him an overflowing house.

The popular instinct was also true to him. The aristocratic classes sneered at his oratorios and complained at his innovations. His music was found to be good bait for the popular gardens and the holiday-makers of the period. Jonathan Tyers was one of the most liberal managers of this class. He was proprietor of Vauxhall Gardens, and Handel (*incognito*) supplied him with nearly all his music. The composer did much the same sort of thing for Marylebone Gardens, furbishing up old and writing new strains with an ease that well became the urgency of the circumstances.

"My grandfather," says the Rev. J. Fountagne, "as I have been told, was an enthusiast in music, and cultivated most of all the friendship of musical men, especially of Handel, who visited him often, and had a great predilection for his society. This leads me to relate an anecdote which I have on the best authority. While Marylebone Gardens were flourishing, the enchanting music of Handel, and probably of Arne, was often heard from the orchestra there. One evening, as my grandfather and Handel were walking together and alone, a new piece was struck up by the band. 'Come, Mr. Fountagne,' said Handel, 'let us sit down and listen to this piece; I want to know your opinion about it.' Down they sat, and after some time the old parson, turning to his companion, said, 'It is not worth listening to; it's very poor stuff.' 'You are right, Mr. Fountagne,' said Handel, 'it is very poor stuff; I thought so myself when I had finished it.' The old gentleman, being taken by surprise, was beginning to apologize; but Handel assured him there was no necessity, that the music was really bad, having been composed hastily, and his time for the production limited; and that the opinion given was as correct as it was honest."

VI.

The period of Handel's highest development had now arrived. For seven years his genius had been slowly but surely maturing, in obedience to the inner law of his being. He had struggled long in the bonds of operatic composition, but even here his innovations showed conclusively how he was reaching out toward the form with which his name was to be associated through all time. The year 1739 was one of prodigious activity. The oratorio of "Saul" was produced, of which the "Dead March" is still recognized as one of the great musical compositions of all time, being one of the few intensely solemn symphonies written in a major key. Several works now forgotten were composed, and the great "Israel in Egypt" was written in the incredibly short space of twenty-seven days. Of this work a distinguished writer on music says: Handel was now fifty-five years old, and had entered, after many a long and weary contest, upon his last and greatest creative period. His genius culminates in the 'Israel.' Elsewhere he has produced longer recitatives and more pathetic arias; nowhere has he written finer tenor songs than 'The enemy said,' or finer duets than 'The Lord is a man of war;' and there is not in the history of music an example of choruses piled up like so many Ossas on Pelions in such majestic strength, and hurled in open defiance at a public whose ears were itching for Italian love-lays and English ballads. In these twenty-eight colossal choruses we perceive at once a reaction against and a triumph over the tastes of the age. The wonder is, not that the 'Israel' was unpopular, but that it should have been tolerated; but Handel, while he appears to have been for years driven by the public, had been, in reality, driving them. His earliest oratorio, 'Il Trionfo del Tempo' (composed in Italy), had but two choruses; into his operas more and more were introduced, with disastrous consequences; but when, at the zenith of his strength, he produced a work which consisted almost entirely of these unpopular peculiarities, the public treated him with respect, and actually sat out three performances in one season! In addition to these two great oratorios, our composer produced the beautiful music to Dryden's "St. Cæcilia Ode," and Milton's "L'Allegro" and "Il Penseroso." Henceforth neither praise nor blame could turn Handel from his appointed course. He was not yet popular with the musical *dilettanti*, but we find no more catering to an absurd taste, no more writing of silly operatic froth.

Our composer had always been very fond of the Irish, and, at the invitation of the lord-lieutenant and prominent Dublin amateurs, he crossed the channel in

1741. He was received with the greatest enthusiasm, and his house became the resort of all the musical people in the city of Dublin. One after another his principal works were produced before admiring audiences in the new Music Hall in Fishamble Street. The crush to hear the "Allegro" and "Penseroso" at the opening performances was so great that the doors had to be closed. The papers declared there never had been seen such a scene before in Dublin.

Handel gave twelve performances at very short intervals, comprising all of his finest works. In these concerts the "Acis and Galatea" and "Alexander's Feast" were the most admired; but the enthusiasm culminated in the rendition of the "Messiah," produced for the first time on April 13, 1742. The performance was a beneficiary one in aid of poor and distressed prisoners for debt in the Marshalsea in Dublin. So, by a remarkable coincidence, the first performance of the "Messiah" literally meant deliverance to the captives. The principal singers were Mrs. Cibber (daughter-in-law of Colley Cibber, and afterward one of the greatest actresses of her time), Mrs. Avoglio, and Mr. Dubourg. The town was wild with excitement. Critics, poets, fine ladies, and men of fashion tore rhetoric to tatters in their admiration. A clergyman so far forgot his Bible in his rapture as to exclaim to Mrs. Cibber, at the close of one of her airs, "Woman, for this be all thy sins forgiven thee." The penny-a-liners wrote that "words were wanting to express the exquisite delight," etc. And—supreme compliment of all, for Handel was a cynical bachelor—the fine ladies consented to leave their hoops at home for the second performance, that a couple of hundred or so extra listeners might be accommodated. This event was the grand triumph of Handel's life. Years of misconception, neglect, and rivalry were swept out of mind in the intoxicating delight of that night's success.

VII.

Handel returned to London, and composed a new oratorio, "Samson," for the following Lenten season. This, together with the "Messiah," heard for the first time in London, made the stock of twelve performances. The fashionable world ignored him altogether; the newspapers kept a contemptuous silence; comic singers were hired to parody his noblest airs at the great houses; and impudent Horace Walpole had the audacity to say that he "had hired all the goddesses from farces and singers of roast-beef, from between the acts of both theatres, with a man with one note in his voice, and a girl with never a one; and so they sang and made brave hallelujahs."

The new field into which Handel had entered inspired his genius to its greatest energy. His new works for the season of 1744 were the "Det-tingen Te Deum," "Semele," and "Joseph and his Brethren;" for the next year (he had again rented the Haymarket Theatre), "Hercules," "Belshazzar," and a revival of "Deborah." All these works were produced in a style of then uncommon completeness, and the great expense he incurred, combined with the active hostility of the fashionable world, forced him to close his doors and suspend payment. From this time forward Handel gave concerts whenever he chose, and depended on the people, who so supported him by their gradually growing appreciation, that in two years he had paid off all his debts, and in ten years had accumulated a fortune of £10,000. The works produced during these latter years were "Judas Maccabæus," 1747; "Alexander," 1748; "Joshua," 1748; "Susannah," 1749; "Solomon," 1749; "Theodora," 1750; "Choice of Hercules," 1751; "Jephthah," 1752, closing with this a stupendous series of dramatic oratorios. While at work on the last, his eyes suffered an attack which finally resulted in blindness.

Like Milton in the case of "Paradise Lost," Handel preferred one of his least popular oratorios, "Theodora." It was a great favorite with him, and he used to say that the chorus, "He saw the lovely youth," was finer than anything in the "Messiah." The public were not of this opinion, and he was glad to give away tickets to any professors who applied for them. When the "Messiah" was again produced, two of these gentlemen who had neglected "Theodora" applied for admission. "Oh! your sarvant, meine Herren!" exclaimed the indignant composer. "You are tamnable dainty! You would not go to 'Theodora'—dere was room enough to dance dere when dat was perform." When Handel heard that an enthusiast had offered to make himself responsible for all the boxes the next time the despised oratorio should be given—"He is a fool," said he; "the Jews will not come to it as to 'Judas Maccabæus,' because it is a Christian story; and the ladies will not come, because it is a virtuous one."

Handel's triumph was now about to culminate in a serene and acknowledged preeminence. The people had recognized his greatness, and the reaction at last conquered all classes. Publishers vied with each other in producing his works, and their performance was greeted with great audiences and enthusiastic applause. His last ten years were a peaceful and beautiful ending of a stormy career.

VIII.

Thought lingers pleasantly over this sunset period. Handel throughout life was so wedded to his art, that he cared nothing for the delights of woman's love. His recreations were simple—rowing, walking, visiting his friends, and playing on the organ. He would sometimes try to play the people out at St. Paul's Cathedral, and hold them indefinitely. He would resort at night to his favorite tavern, the "Queen's Head," where he would smoke and drink beer with his chosen friends. Here he would indulge in roaring conviviality and fun, and delight his friends with sparkling satire and pungent humor, of which he was a great master, helped by his amusing compound of English, Italian, and German. Often he would visit the picture galleries, of which he was passionately fond. His clumsy but noble figure could be seen almost any morning rolling through Charing Cross; and every one who met old Father Handel treated him with the deepest reverence.

The following graphic narrative, taken from the "Somerset House Gazette," offers a vivid portraiture. Schoelcher, in his "Life of Handel," says that "its author had a relative, Zachary Hardcastle, a retired merchant, who was intimately acquainted with all the most distinguished men of his time, artists, poets, musicians, and physicians." This old gentleman, who lived at Paper Buildings, was accustomed to take his morning walk in the garden of Somerset House, where he happened to meet with another old man, Colley Cibber, and proposed to him to go and hear a competition which was to take place at midday for the post of organist to the Temple, and he invited him to breakfast, telling him at the same time that Dr. Pepusch and Dr. Arne were to be with him at nine o'clock. They go in; Pepusch arrives punctually at the stroke of nine; presently there is a knock, the door is opened, and Handel unexpectedly presents himself. Then follows the scene:

"Handel: 'Vat! mein dear friend Hardgasdle—vat! you are merry py dimes! Vat! and Misder Golley Cibbers too! ay, and Togder Peepbush as veil! Vell, dat is gomigal. Veil, mein friendts, andt how vags the vorldt wid you, mein tdears? Bray, bray, do let me sit town a momend.'

"Pepusch took the great man's hat, Colley Cibber took his stick, and my great-uncle wheeled round his reading-chair, which was somewhat about the dimensions of that in which our kings and queens are crowned; and then the great man sat him down.

"'Vell, I thank you, gentlemen; now I am at mein ease vonce more. Upon mein vord, dat is a picture of a ham. It is very pold of me to gome to preak my fastd wid you uninvited; and I have brought along wid me a nodable abbetite; for the wader of old Fader Dems is it not a fine pracer of the stomach?'

"'You do me great honor, Mr. Handel,' said my great-uncle. 'I take this early visit as a great kindness.'

"'A delightful morning for the water,' said Colley Cibber.

"'Pray, did you come with oars or scullers, Mr. Handel?' said Pepusch.

"'Now, how gan you demand of me dat zilly question, you who are a musician and a man of science, Togder Peepbush? Vat gan it concern you whether I have one votdermans or two votd-ermans—whether I bull out mine burce for to pay von shilling or two? Diavolo! I gannot go here, or I gannot go dere, but some one shall send it to some newsbaber, as how Misder Chorge Vreder-ick Handel did go sometimes last week in a votderman's wherry, to preak his fastd wid Misder Zac. Hardgasdle; but it shall be all the fault wid himself, if it shall be but in print, whether I was rowed by one votdermans or by two votdermans. So, Togder Peepbush, you will blease to excuse me from dat.'

"Poor Dr. Pepusch was for a moment disconcerted, but it was soon forgotten in the first dish of coffee.

"'Well, gentlemen,' said my great-uncle Zachary, looking at his tompion, 'it is ten minutes past nine. Shall we wait more for Dr. Arne?"

"'Let us give him another five minutes' chance, Master Hardcastle,' said Colley Cibber; 'he is too great a genius to keep time.'

"'Let us put it to the vote,' said Dr. Pepusch, smiling. 'Who holds up hands?'

"'I will segond your motion wid all mine heardt,' said Handel. 'I will hold up mine feeble hands for mine oldt friendt Custos (Arne's name was Augustine), for I know not who I wouldt waidt for, over andt above mine oldt rival, Master Dom (meaning Pepusch). Only by your bermission, I vill dake a snag of your ham, andt a slice of French roll, or a modicum of chicken; for to dell you the honest fagd, I am all pote famished, for I laid me down on mine billow in bed the lastd nightd widout mine supper, at the instance of mine physician, for which I am not altogeddere inglined to extend mine fastd no longer.' Then, laughing: 'Berhaps, Mister Golley Cibbers, you may like to pote this to the vote? But I shall not segond the motion, nor shall I holdt up mine hand, as I will, by bermission, embloy it some dime in a better office. So, if you blease, do me the kindness for to gut me a small slice of ham.'

"At this instant a hasty footstep was heard on the stairs, accompanied by the humming of an air, all as gay as the morning, which was beautiful and bright. It was the month of May.

"'Bresto! be quick,' said Handel; he knew it was Arne; 'fifteen minutes of dime is butty well for an *ad libitum*.'

"'Mr. Arne,' said my great-uncle's man.

"A chair was placed, and the social party commenced their déjeuner.

"'Well, and how do you find yourself, my dear sir?' inquired Arne, with friendly warmth.

"'Why, by the mercy of Heaven, and the waders of Aix-la-Chapelle, andt the addentions of mine togders andt physicians, and oggulists, of lade years, under Providence, I am surbrizingly pedder—thank you kindly, Misder Custos. Andt you have also been doing well of lade, as I am bleased to hear. You see, sir,' pointing to his plate, 'you see, sir, dat I am in the way for to regruit mine flesh wid the good viands of Misder Zachary Hardgasdle.'

"'So, sir, I presume you are come to witness the trial of skill at the old round church? I understand the amateurs expect a pretty sharp contest,' said Arne.

"'Gondest,' echoed Handel, laying down his knife and fork. 'Yes, no doubt; your amadeurs have a bassion for gondest. Not vot it vos in our remembrance. Hey, mine friendt? Ha, ha, ha!'

"'No, sir, I am happy to say those days of envy and bickering, and party feeling, are gone and past. To be sure we had enough of such disgraceful warfare: it lasted too long.'

"'Why, yes; it tid last too long, it bereft me of mine poor limbs: it tid bereave of that vot is the most blessed gift of Him vot made us, andt not wee ourselves. And for vot? Vy, for nod-ing in the vorldt pode the bleasure and bastime of them who, having no widt, nor no want, set at loggerheads such men as live by their widts, to worry and destroy one andt anodere as wild beasts in the Golloseum in the dimes of the Romans.'

"Poor Dr. Pepusch during this conversation, as my great-uncle observed, was sitting on thorns; he was in the confederacy professionally only.

"'I hope, sir,' observed the doctor, 'you do not include me among those who did injustice to your talents?'

"'Nod at all, nod at all, God forbid! I am a great admirer of the airs of the 'Peggar's Obéra,' andt every professional gendtleman must do his best for to live.'

"This mild return, couched under an apparent compliment, was well received; but Handel, who had a talent for sarcastic drolling, added:

"'Pute why blay the Peggar yourself, togder, andt adapt oldt pallad humsdrum, ven, as a man of science, you could gombose original airs of your own? Here is mine friendt, Custos Arne, who has made a road for himself, for to drive along his own genius to the demple of fame.' Then, turning to our illustrious Arne, he continued, 'Min friendt Custos, you and I must meed togeder some dimes before it is long, and hold a *têde-à-têde* of old days vat is gone; ha, ha! Oh! it is gomigal now dat id is all gone by. Custos, to nod you remember as it was almost only of yesterday dat she-devil Guzzoni, andt dat other brecious taugh-ter of iniquity, Pelzebub's spoiled child, the bretty-f aced Faustina? Oh! the mad rage vot I have to answer for, vot with one and the oder of these fine latdies' airs andt graces. Again, to you nod remember dat ubstardt buppy Senesino, and the goxgomb Farinelli? Next, again, mine some-dimes nodtable rival Bononcini, and old Borbora? Ha, ha, ha! all at war wid me, andt all at war wid themselves. Such a gonfusion of rivalshibs, andt double-facedness, andt hybocrisy, and malice, vot would make a gomigal subject for a boem in rhymes, or a biece for the stage, as I hopes to be saved.'"

IX.

We now turn from the man to his music. In his daily life with the world we get a spectacle of a quick, passionate temper, incased in a great burly frame, and raging into whirlwinds of excitement at small provocation; a gourmand devoted to the pleasure of the table, sometimes indeed gratifying his appetite in no seemly fashion, resembling his friend Dr. Samuel Johnson in many notable ways. Handel as a man was of the earth, earthy, in the extreme, and marked by many whimsical and disagreeable faults. But in his art we recognize a genius so colossal, massive, and self-poised as to raise admiration to its superlative of awe. When Handel had disencumbered himself of tradition, convention, the trappings of time and circumstance, he attained a place in musical creation, solitary and unique. His genius found expression in forms large and austere, disdaining the luxuriant and trivial. He embodied the spirit of Protestantism in music; and a recognition of this fact is probably the key of the admiration felt for him by the Anglo-Saxon races.

Handel possessed an inexhaustible fund of melody of the noblest order; an almost unequaled command of musical expression; perfect power over all the resources of his science; the faculty of wielding huge masses of tone with perfect ease and felicity; and he was without rival in the sublimity of ideas. The problem which he so successfully solved in the oratorio was that of giving such dramatic force to the music, in which he clothed the sacred texts, as to be able to dispense with all scenic and stage effects. One of the finest operatic composers of the time, the rival of Bach as an instrumental composer, and performer on the harpsichord or organ, the unanimous verdict of the musical world is that no one has ever equaled him in completeness, range of effect, elevation and variety of conception, and sublimity in the treatment of sacred music. We can readily appreciate Handel's own words when describing his own sensations in writing the "Messiah:" "I did think I did see all heaven before me, and the great God himself."

The great man died on Good Friday night, 1759, aged seventy-five years. He had often wished "he might breathe his last on Good Friday, in hope," he said, "of meeting his good God, his sweet Lord and Saviour, on the day of his resurrection." The old blind musician had his wish.

GLUCK

Gluck is a noble and striking figure in musical history, alike in the services he rendered to his art and the dignity and strength of his personal character. As the predecessor of Wagner and Meyerbeer, who among the composers of this century have given opera its largest and noblest expression, he anticipated their important reforms, and in his musical creations we see all that is best in what is called the new school.

The man, the Ritter Christoph Wilibald von Gluck, is almost as interesting to us as the musician. He moved in the society of princes with a calm and haughty dignity, their conscious peer, and never prostituted his art to gain personal advancement or to curry favor with the great ones of the earth. He possessed a majesty of nature which was the combined effect of personal pride, a certain lofty self-reliance, and a deep conviction that he was the apostle of an important musical mission.

Gluck's whole life was illumined by an indomitable sense of his own strength, and lifted by it into an atmosphere high above that of his rivals, whom, the world has now almost forgotten, except as they were immortalized by being his enemies. Like Milton and Bacon, who put on record their knowledge that they had written for all time, Gluck had a magnificent consciousness of himself. "I have written," he says, "the music of my 'Ar-mida' in such a manner as to prevent its soon growing old." This is a sublime vanity inseparable from the great aggressive geniuses of the world, the wind of the speed which measures their force of impact.

Duplessis's portrait of Gluck almost takes the man out of paint to put him in flesh and blood. He looks down with wide-open eyes, swelling nostrils, firm mouth, and massive chin. The noble brow, dome-like and expanded, relieves the massiveness of his face; and the whole countenance and figure express the repose of a powerful and passionate nature schooled into balance and symmetry: altogether the presentment of a great man, who felt that he could move the world and had found the *pou sto*. Of a large and robust type of physical beauty, Nature seems to have endowed him on every hand with splendid gifts. Such a man as this could say with calm simplicity to Marie Antoinette, who inquired one night about his new opera of "Armida," then nearly finished: "*Madame, il est bientôt fini, et vraiment ce sera superbe.*"

One night Handel listened to a new opera from a young and unknown composer, the "Caduta de' Giganti," one of Gluck's very earliest works, written when he was yet corrupted with all the vices of the Italian method. "Mein Gott!

he is an idiot," said Handel; "he knows no more of counterpoint then mein cook." Handel did not see with prophetic eyes. He never met Gluck afterward, and we do not know his later opinion of the composer of "Orpheus and Eurydice" and "Iphigenia in Tauris." But Gluck had ever the profoundest admiration for the author of the "Messiah." There was something in these two strikingly similar, as their music was alike characterized by massive simplicity and strength, not rough-hewn, but shaped into austere beauty.

Before we relate the great episode of our composer's life, let us take a backward glance at his youth. He was the son of a forester in the service of Prince Lobkowitz born at Weidenwang in the Upper Palatinate, July 2,1714. Gluck was devoted to music from early childhood, but received, in connection with the musical art, an excellent education at the Jesuit College of Kommotau. Here he learned singing, the organ, the violin and harpsichord, and had a mind to get his living by devoting his musical talents to the Church. The Prague public recognized in him a musician of fair talent, but he found but little encouragement to stay at the Bohemian capital. So he decided to finish his musical education at Vienna, where more distinguished masters could be had. Prince Lobkowitz, who remembered his gamekeeper's son, introduced the young man to the Italian Prince Melzi, who induced him to accompany him to Milan. As the pupil of the Italian organist and composer, Sammartini, he made rapid progress in operatic composition. He was successful in pleasing Italian audiences, and in four years produced eight operas, for which the world has forgiven him in forgetting them. Then Gluck must go to London to see what impression he could make on English critics; for London then, as now, was one of the great musical centres, where every successful composer or singer must get his brevet.

Gluck's failure to please in London was, perhaps, an important epoch in his career. With a mind singularly sensitive to new impressions, and already struggling with fresh ideas in the laws of operatic composition, Handel's great music must have had a powerful effect in stimulating his unconscious progress. His last production in England, "Pyramus and Thisbe," was a *pasticcio* opera, in which he embodied the best bits out of his previous works. The experiment was a glaring failure, as it ought to have been; for it illustrated the Italian method, which was designed for mere vocal display, carried to its logical absurdity.

II.

In 1748 Gluck settled in Vienna, where almost immediately his opera of "Semiramide" was produced. Here he conceived a passion for Marianne, the daughter of Joseph Pergin, a rich banker; but on account of the father's distaste for a musical son-in-law, the marriage did not occur till 1750. "Telemacco" and "Clemenza di Tito" were composed about this time, and performed in Vienna, Rome, and Naples. In 1755 our composer received the order of the Golden Spur from the Roman pontiff in recognition of the merits of two operas performed at Rome, called "Il Trionfo di Camillo" and "Antigono." Seven years were now actively employed in producing operas for Vienna and Italian cities, which, without possessing great value, show the change which had begun to take place in this composer's theories of dramatic music. In Paris he had been struck with the operas of Rameau, in which the declamatory form was strongly marked. His early Italian training had fixed in his mind the importance of pure melody. From Germany he obtained his appreciation of harmony, and had made a deep study of the uses of the orchestra. So we see this great reformer struggling on with many faltering steps toward that result which he afterward summed up in the following concise description: "My purpose was to restrict music to its true office, that of ministering to the expression of poetry, without interrupting the action."

In Calzabigi Gluck had met an author who fully appreciated his ideas, and had the talent of writing a libretto in accordance with them. This coadjutor wrote all the librettos that belonged to Gluck's greatest period. He had produced his "Orpheus and Eurydice" and "Alceste" in Vienna with a fair amount of success; but his tastes drew him strongly to the French stage, where the art of acting and declamation was cultivated then, as it is now, to a height unknown in other parts of Europe. So we find him gladly accepting an offer from the managers of the French Opera to migrate to the great city, in which were fermenting with much noisy fervor those new ideas in art, literature, politics, and society, which were turning the eyes of all Europe to the French capital.

The world's history has hardly a more picturesque and striking spectacle, a period more fraught with the working of powerful forces, than that exhibited by French society in the latter part of Louis XV.'s reign. We see a court rotten to the core with indulgence in every form of sensuality and vice, yet glittering with the veneer of a social polish which made it the admiration of the world. A dissolute king was ruled by a succession of mistresses, and all the courtiers vied in emulating the vice and extravagance of their master. Yet in this foul compost-heap art and literature nourished with a tropical luxuriance. Voltaire was at the height of his splendid career, the most brilliant wit and philosopher of his age. The lightnings of his mockery attacked with an incessant play the social, political, and religious shams of the period. People of all classes, under the influence of his unsparing satire, were learning to see with clear eyes what an utterly artificial and polluted age they lived in, and the cement which bound society in a compact whole was fast melting under this powerful solvent.

Rousseau, with his romantic philosophy and eloquence, had planted his new ideas deep in the hearts of his contemporaries, weary with the artifice and the corruption of a time which had exhausted itself and had nothing to promise under the old social *regime*. The ideals uplifted in the "Nouvelle Héloïse" and the "Confessions" awakened men's minds with a great rebound to the charms of Nature, simplicity, and a social order untrammeled by rules or conventions. The eloquence with which these theories were propounded carried the French people by storm, and Rousseau was a demigod at whose shrine worshiped alike duchess and peasant. The Encyclopedists stimulated the ferment by their literary enthusiasm, and the heartiness with which they cooperated with the whole current of revolutionary thought.

The very atmosphere was reeking with the prophecy of imminent change.

Versailles itself did not escape the contagion. Courtiers and aristocrats, in worshiping the beautiful ideals set up by the new school, which were as far removed as possible from their own effete civilization, did not realize that they were playing with the fire which was to burn out the whole social edifice of France with such a terrible conflagration; for, back and beneath all this, there was a people groaning under long centuries of accumulated wrong, in whose imbruted hearts the theories applauded by their oppressors with a sort of *doctrinaire* delight were working with a fatal fever.

III.

In this strange condition of affairs Gluck found his new sphere of labor— Gluck, himself overflowing with the revolutionary spirit, full of the enthusiasm of reform. At first he carried everything before him. Protected by royalty, he produced, on the basis of an admirable libretto by Du Rollet, one of the great wits of the time, "Iphigenia in Aulis." It was enthusiastically received. The critics, delighted to establish the reputation of one especially favored by the Dau-phiness Marie Antoinette, exhausted superlatives on the new opera. The Abbé Arnaud, one of the leading *dilettanti*, exclaimed: "With such music one might found a new religion!" To be sure, the connoisseurs could not understand the complexities of the music; but, following the rule of all connoisseurs before or since, they considered it all the more learned and profound. So led, the general public clapped their hands, and agreed to consider Gluck as a great composer. He was called the Hercules of music; the opera-house was crammed night after night; his footsteps were dogged in the streets by admiring enthusiasts; the wits and poets occupied themselves with composing sonnets in his praise; brilliant courtiers and fine ladies showered valuable gifts on the new musical oracle; he was hailed as the exponent of Rousseauism in music. We read that it was considered to be a priceless privilege to be admitted to the rehearsal of a new opera, to see Gluck conduct in nightcap and dressing-gown.

Fresh adaptations of "Orpheus and Eurydice" and of "Alceste" were produced. The first, brought out in 1784, was received with an enthusiasm which could be contented only with forty-nine consecutive performances. The second act of this work has been called one of the most astonishing productions of the human mind. The public began to show signs of fickleness, however, on the production of the "Alceste." On the first night a murmur arose among the spectators: "The piece has fallen." Abbé Arnaud, Gluck's devoted defender, arose in his box and replied: "Yes! fallen from heaven." While Mademoiselle Levasseur was singing one of the great airs, a voice was heard to say, "Ah! you tear out my ears;" to which the caustic rejoinder was: "How fortunate, if it is to give you others!"

Gluck himself was badly bitten, in spite of his hatred of shams and shallowness, with the pretenses of the time, which professed to dote on nature and simplicity. In a letter to his old pupil, Marie Antoinette, wherein he disclaims any pretension of teaching the French a new school of music, he says: "I see with satisfaction that the language of Nature is the universal language."

So, here on the crumbling crust of a volcano, where the volatile French court danced and fiddled and sang, unreckoning of what was soon to come, our composer and his admirers patted each other on the back with infinite complacency.

But after this high tide of prosperity there was to come a reverse. A powerful faction, that for a time had been crushed by Gluck's triumph, after a while raised their heads and organized an attack. There were second-rate composers whose scores had been laid on the shelf in the rage for the new favorite; musicians who were shocked and enraged at the difficulties of his instrumentation; wits who, having praised Gluck for a while, thought they could now find a readier field for their quills in satire; and a large section of the public who changed for no earthly reason but that they got tired of doing one thing.

Therefore, the Italian Piccini was imported to be pitted against the reigning deity. The French court was broken up into hostile ranks. Marie Antoinette was Gluck's patron, but Madame Du Barry, the king's mistress, declared for Piccini. Abbé Arnaud fought for Gluck; but the witty Marmontel was the advocate of his rival. The keen-witted Du Rollet was Gluckist; but La Harpe, the eloquent, was Piccinist. So this battle-royal in art commenced and raged with virulence. The green-room was made unmusical with contentions carried out in polite Billingsgate. Gluck tore up his unfinished score in rage when he learned that his rival was to compose an opera on the same libretto. La Harpe said: "The famous Gluck may puff his own compositions, but he can't prevent them from boring us to death." Thus the wags of Paris laughed and wrangled over the musical rivals. Berton, the new director, fancied he could soften the dispute and make the two composers friends; so at a dinner-party, when they were all in their cups, he proposed that they should compose an opera jointly. This was demurred to; but it was finally arranged that they should compose an opera on the same subject.

"Iphigenia in Tauris," Gluck's second "Iphigenia," produced in 1779, was such a masterpiece that his rival shut his own score in his portfolio, and kept it two years. All Paris was enraptured with this great work, and Gluck's detractors were silenced in the wave of enthusiasm which swept the public. Abbé Arnaud's opinion was the echo of the general mind: "There was but one beautiful part, and that was the whole of it." This opera may be regarded as the most perfect example of Gluck's school in making the music the full reflex of the dramatic action. While Orestes sings in the opera, "My heart is calm," the orchestra continues to paint the agitation of his thoughts. During the rehearsal the musician failed to understand the exigency and ceased playing. The composer cried out, in a rage: "Don't you see he is lying? Go on, go on; he as just killed his mother." On one occasion, when he was praising Rameau's chorus of "Castor and Pollux," an admirer of his flattered him with the remark, "But what a difference between this chorus and that of your 'Iphigénie'!" "Yet it is very well done," said Gluck; "one is only a religious ceremony, the other is a real funeral." He was wont to say that in composing he always tried to forget he was a musician.

Gluck, however, a few months subsequent to this, was so much humiliated at the non-success of "Echo and Narcissus," that he left Paris in bitter irritation, in spite of Marie Antoinette's pleadings that he should remain at the French capital.

The composer was now advanced in years, and had become impatient and fretful. He left Paris for Vienna in 1780, having amassed considerable property. There, as an old, broken-down man, he listened to the young Mozart's new symphonies and operas, and applauded them with great zeal; for Gluck, though fiery and haughty in the extreme, was singularly generous in recognizing the merits of others.

This was exhibited in Paris in his treatment of Méhul, the Belgian composer, then a youth of sixteen, who had just arrived in the gay city. It was on the eve of the first representation of "Iphigenia in Tauris," when the operatic battle was agitating the public. With all the ardor of a novice and a devotee, the young musical student immediately threw himself into the affray, and by the aid of a friend he succeeded in gaining admittance to the theatre for the final rehearsal of Gluck's opera. This so enchanted him that he resolved to be present at the public performance. But, unluckily for the resolve, he had no money, and no prospect of obtaining any; so, with a determination and a love for art which deserve to be remembered, he decided to hide himself in one of the boxes and there to wait for the time of representation.

"At the end of the rehearsal," writes George Hogarth in his "Memoirs of the Drama," "he was discovered in his place of concealment by the servants of the theatre, who proceeded to turn him out very roughly. Gluck, who had not left the house, heard the noise, came to the spot, and found the young man, whose spirit was roused, resisting the indignity with which he was treated. Méhul, finding in whose presence he was, was ready to sink with confusion; but, in answer to Gluck's questions, he told him that he was a young musical student from the country, whose anxiety to be present at the performance of the opera had led him into the commission of an impropriety. Gluck, as may be supposed, was delighted with a piece of enthusiasm so flattering to himself, and not only gave his young admirer a ticket of admission, but desired his acquaintance." From this artistic *contretemps*, then, arose a friendship alike creditable to the goodness and generosity of Gluck, as it was to the sincerity and high order of Méhul's musical talent.

Gluck's death, in 1787, was caused by overindulgence in wine at a dinner which he gave to some of his friends. The love of stimulants had grown upon him in his old age, and had become almost a passion. An enforced abstinence of some months was succeeded by a debauch, in which he drank an immense quantity of brandy. The effects brought on a fit of apoplexy, of which he died, aged seventy-three.

Gluck's place in musical history is peculiar and well marked, he entered the field of operatic composition when it was hampered with a great variety of dry forms, and utterly without soul and poetic spirit. The object of composers seemed to be to show mere contrapuntal learning, or to furnish singers opportunity to display vocal agility. The opera, as a large and symmetrical expression of human emotions, suggested in the collisions of a dramatic story, was utterly an unknown quantity in art. Gluck's attention was early called to this radical inconsistency; and, though he did not learn for many years to develop his musical ideas according to a theory, and never carried that theory to the logical results insisted on by his great after-type, Wagner, he accomplished much in the way of sweeping reform. He elaborated the recitative or declamatory element in opera with great care, and insisted that his singers should make this the object of their most careful efforts. The arias, duos, quartets, etc., as well as the choruses and orchestral parts, were made consistent with the dramatic motive and situations. In a word, Gluck aimed with a single-hearted purpose to make music the expression of poetry and sentiment.

The principles of Gluck's school of operatic writing may be briefly summarized as follows: That dramatic music can only reach its highest power and beauty when joined to a simple and poetic text, expressing passions true to Nature; that music can be made the language of all the varied emotions of the heart; that the music of an opera must exactly follow the rhythm and melody of the words; that the orchestra must be only used to strengthen and intensify the feeling embodied in the vocal parts, as demanded by the text or dramatic situation. We get some further light on these principles from Gluck's letter of dedication to the Grand-Duke of Tuscany on the publication of "Alceste." He writes: "I am of opinion that music must be to poetry what liveliness of color and a happy mixture of light and shade are for a faultless and well-arranged drawing, which serve to add life to the figures without injuring the outlines;... that the overture should prepare the auditors for the character of the action which is to be presented, and hint at the progress of the same; that the instruments must be employed according to the degree of interest and passion; that the composer should avoid too marked a disparity in the dialogue-between the air and recitative, in order not to break the sense of a period, or interrupt the energy of the action.... Finally, I have even felt compelled to sacrifice rules to the improvement of the effect."

We find in this composer's music, therefore, a largeness and dignity of treatment which have never been surpassed. His command of melody is quite remarkable, but his use of it is under severe artistic restraint; for it is always characterized by breadth, simplicity, and directness. He aimed at and attained the symmetrical balance of an old Greek play.

HAYDN.

I.

"Papa Haydn!" Thus did Mozart ever speak of his foster-father in music, and the title, transmitted to posterity, admirably expressed the sweet, placid, gentle nature, whose possessor was personally beloved no less than he was admired. His life flowed, broad and unruffled, like some great river, unvexed for the most part by the rivalries, jealousies, and sufferings, oftentimes self-inflicted, which have harassed the careers of other great musicians. He remained to the last the favorite of the imperial court of Vienna, and princes followed his remains to their last resting-place.

Joseph Haydn was the eldest of the twenty children of Matthias Haydn, a wheelwright at Rohrau, Lower Austria, where he was born in 1732. At the age of twelve years he was engaged to sing in Vienna. He became a chorister in St. Stephen's Church, but offended the choir-master by the revolt on the part of himself and parents from submitting to the usual means then taken to perpetuate a fine soprano in boys. So Haydn, who had surreptitiously picked up a good deal of musical knowledge apart from the art of singing, was at the age of sixteen turned out on the world. A compassionate barber, however, took him in, and Haydn dressed and powdered wigs down-stairs, while he worked away at a little worm-eaten harpsichord at night in his room. Unfortunate boy! he managed to get himself engaged to the barber's daughter, Anne Keller, who was for a good while the Xantippe of his gentle life, and he paid dearly for his father-in-law's early hospitality.

The young musician soon began to be known, as he played the violin in one church, the organ in another, and got some pupils. His first rise was his acquaintance with Metastasio, the poet laureate of the court. Through him, Haydn got introduced to the mistress of the Venetian embassador, a great musical enthusiast, and in her circle he met Porpora, the best music-master in the world, but a crusty, snarling old man. Porpora held at Vienna the position of musical dictator and censor, and he exercised the tyrannical privileges of his post mercilessly. Haydn was a small, dark-complexioned, insignificant-looking youth, and Porpora, of course, snubbed him most contemptuously. But Haydn wanted instruction, and no one in the world could give it so well as the savage old *maestro*. So he performed all sorts of menial services for him, cleaned his shoes, powdered his wig, and ran all his errands. The result was that Porpora softened and consented to give his young admirer lessons—no great hardship, for young Haydn proved a most apt and gifted pupil. And it was not long either before the young musician's compositions attracted public attention and found a sale. The very curious relations between Haydn and Porpora are brilliantly sketched in George Sand's "Consuelo."

At night Haydn, accompanied by his friends, was wont to wander about Vienna by moonlight, and serenade his patrons with trios and quartets of his own composition. He happened one night to stop under the window of Bernardone Kurz, a director of a theatre and the leading clown of Vienna. Down rushed Kurz very excitedly. "Who are you?" he shrieked. "Joseph Haydn." "Whose music is it?" "Mine." "The deuce it is! And at your age, too!" "Why, I must begin with something." "Come along up-stairs."

The enthusiastic director collared his prize, and was soon deep in explaining a wonderful libretto, entitled "The Devil on Two Sticks." To write music for this was no easy matter; for it was to represent all sorts of absurd things, among others a tempest. The tempest made Haydn despair, and he sat at the piano, banging away in a reckless fashion, while the director stood behind him, raving in a disconnected way as to his meaning. At last the distracted pianist brought his fists simultaneously down upon the key-board, and made a rapid sweep of all the notes.

"Bravo! bravo! that is the tempest!" cried Kurz.

The buffoon also laid himself on a chair, and had it carried about the room, during which he threw out his limbs in imitation of the act of swimming. Haydn supplied an accompaniment so suitable that Kurz soon landed on *terra firma*, and congratulated the composer, assuring him that he was the man to compose the opera. By this stroke of good luck our young musician received one hundred and thirty florins.

II.

At the age of twenty-eight Haydn composed his first symphony. Soon after this he attracted the attention of the old Prince Esterhazy, all the members of whose family have become known in the history of music as generous Mæcenases of the art.

"What! you don't mean to say that little blackamoor" (alluding to Haydn's brown complexion and small stature) "composed that symphony?"

"Surely, prince," replied the director Friedburg, beckoning to Joseph Haydn, who advanced toward the orchestra.

"Little Moor," says the old gentleman, "you shall enter my service. I am Prince Esterhazy. What's your name?"

"Haydn."

"Ah! I've heard of you. Get along and dress yourself like a *Kapellmeister*. Clap on a new coat, and mind your wig is curled. You're too short. You shall have red heels; but they shall be high, that your stature may correspond with your merit."

So he went to live at Eisenstadt in the Esterhazy household, and received a salary of four hundred florins, which was afterward raised to one thousand by Prince Nicholas Esterhazy. Haydn continued the intimate friend and associate of Prince Nicholas for thirty years, and death only dissolved the bond between them. In the Esterhazy household the life of Haydn was a very quiet one, a life of incessant and happy industry; for he poured out an incredible number of works, among them not a few of his most famous ones. So he spent a happy life in hard labor, alternated with delightful recreations at the Esterhazy country-seat, mountain rambles, hunting and fishing, open-air concerts, musical evenings, etc.

A French traveler who visited Esterhaz about 1782 says: "The château stands quite solitary, and the prince sees nobody but his officials and servants, and strangers who come hither from curiosity. He has a puppet-theatre, which is certainly unique in character. Here the grandest operas are produced. One knows not whether to be amazed or to laugh at seeing 'Alceste,' 'Alcides,' etc., put on the stage with all due solemnity and played by puppets. His orchestra is one of the best I ever heard, and the great Hadyn is his court and theatre composer. He employs a poet for his singular theatre, whose humor and skill in suiting the grandest subjects for the stage, and in parodying the gravest effects, are often exceedingly happy. He often engages a troupe of wandering players for months at a time, and he himself and his retinue form the entire audience. They are allowed to come on the stage uncombed, drunk, their parts not half learned, and half dressed. The prince is not for the serious and tragic, and he enjoys it when the players, like Sancho Panza, give loose reins to their humor."

Yet Haydn was not perfectly contented. He would have been had it not been for his terrible wife, the hair-dresser's daughter, who had a dismal, mischievous, sullen nature, a venomous tongue, and a savage temper. She kept Haydn in hot water continually, till at last he broke loose from this plague by separating from her. Scandal says that Haydn, who had a very affectionate and sympathetic nature, found ample consolation for marital infelicity in the charms and society of the lovely Boselli, a great singer. He had her picture painted, and humored all her whims and caprices, to the sore depletion of his pocket.

In after-years again he was mixed up in a little affair with the great Mrs. Billington, whose beautiful person was no less marked than her fine voice. Sir Joshua Reynolds was painting her portrait for him, and had represented her as St. Cecilia listening to celestial music. Haydn paid her a charming compliment at one of the sittings.

"What do you think of the charming Billington's picture?" said Sir Joshua.

"Yes," said Haydn, "it is indeed a beautiful picture. It is just like her, but there's a strange mistake."

"What is that?"

"Why, you have painted her listening to the angels, when you ought to have painted the angels listening to her."

At one time, during Haydn's connection with Prince Esterhazy, the latter, from motives of economy, determined to dismiss his celebrated orchestra, which he supported at great expense. Haydn was the leader, and his patron's purpose caused him sore pain, as indeed it did all the players, among whom were many distinguished instrumentalists. Still, there was nothing to be done but for all concerned to make themselves as cheerful as possible under the circumstances; so, with that fund of wit and humor which seems to have been concealed under the immaculate coat and formal wig of the straitlaced Haydn, he set about composing a work for the last performance of the royal band, a work which has ever since borne the appropriate title of the "Farewell Symphony."

On the night appointed for the last performance a brilliant company, including the prince, had assembled. The music of the new symphony began gayly enough —it was even merry. As it went on, however, it became soft and dreamy. The strains were sad and "long drawn out." At length a sorrowful wailing began. One instrument after another left off, and each musician, as his task ended, blew out his lamp and departed with his music rolled up under his arm.

Haydn was the last to finish, save one, and this was the prince's favorite violinist, who said all that he had to say in a brilliant violin cadenza, when, behold! he made off.

The prince was astonished. "What is the meaning of all this?" cried he.

"It is our sorrowful farewell," answered Haydn.

This was too much. The prince was overcome, and, with a good laugh, said:

"Well, I think I must reconsider my decision. At any rate, we will not say 'good-by' now."

III.

During the thirty years of Haydn's quiet life with the Esterhazys he had been gradually acquiring an immense reputation in France, England, and Spain, of which he himself was unconscious. His great symphonies had stamped him worldwide as a composer of remarkable creative genius. Haydn's modesty prevented him from recognizing his own celebrity. Therefore, we can fancy his astonishment when, shortly after the death of Prince Nicholas Esterhazy, a stranger called on him and said: "I am Salomon, from London, and must strike a bargain with you for that city immediately."

Haydn was dazed with the suddenness of the proposition, but the old ties were broken up, and his grief needed recreation and change. Still, he had many beloved friends, whose society it was hard to leave. Chief among these was Mozart. "Oh, papa," said Mozart, "you have had no training for the wide world, and you speak so few languages." "Oh, my language is understood all over the world," said Papa Haydn, with a smile. When he departed for England, December 15, 1790, Mozart could with difficulty tear himself away, and said, with pathetic tears, "We shall doubtless now take our last farewell."

Haydn and Mozart were perfectly in accord, and each thought and did well toward the other. Mozart, we know, was born when Haydn had just reached manhood, so that when Mozart became old enough to study composition the earlier works of Haydn's chamber music had been written; and these undoubtedly formed the studies of the boy Mozart, and greatly influenced his style; so that Haydn was the model and, in a sense, the instructor of Mozart. Strange is it then to find, in after-years, the master borrowing (perhaps with interest!) from the pupil. Such, however, was the fact, as every amateur knows. At this we can hardly wonder, for Haydn possessed unbounded admiration not only for Mozart, but also for his music, which the following shows. Being asked by a friend at Prague to send him an opera, he replied:

"With all my heart, if you desire to have it for yourself alone, but if you wish to perform it in public, I must be excused; for, being written specially for my company at the Esterhazy Palace, it would not produce the proper effect elsewhere. I would do a new score for your theatre; but what a hazardous step it would be to stand in comparison with Mozart! Oh, Mozart! If I could instill into the soul of every lover of music the admiration I have for his matchless works, all countries would seek to be possessed of so great a treasure. Let Prague keep him, ah! and well reward him, for without that the history of geniuses is bad; alas! we see so many noble minds crushed beneath adversity. Mozart is incomparable, and I am annoyed that he is unable to obtain any court appointment. Forgive me if I get excited when speaking of him, I am so fond of him."

Mozart's admiration for Haydn's music, too, was very marked. He and Herr Kozeluch were one day listening to a composition of Haydn's which contained some bold modulations. Kozeluch thought them strange, and asked Mozart whether he would have written them. "I think not," smartly replied Mozart, "and for this reason: because they would not have occurred either to you or me!"

On another occasion we find Mozart taking to task a Viennese professor of some celebrity, who used to experience great delight in turning to Haydn's compositions to find therein any evidence of the master's want of sound theoretical training—a quest in which the pedant occasionally succeeded. One day he came to Mozart with a great crime to unfold. Mozart as usual endeavored to turn the conversation, but the learned professor still went chattering on, till at last Mozart shut his mouth with the following pill: "Sir, if you and I were both melted down together, we should not furnish materials for one Haydn."

It was one of the most beautiful friendships in the history of art; full of tender offices, and utterly free from the least taint of envy or selfishness.

IV.

Haydn landed in England after a voyage which delighted him in spite of his terror of the sea—a feeling which seems to be usual among people of very high musical sensibilities. In his diary we find recorded: "By four o'clock we had come twenty miles. The large vessel stood out to sea five hours longer, till the tide carried it into the harbor. I remained on deck the whole passage, in order to gaze my fill at that huge monster—the ocean."

The novelty of Haydn's concerts—of which he was to give twenty at fifty pounds apiece—consisted of their being his own symphonies, conducted by himself in person. Haydn's name, during his serene, uneventful years with the Ester-hazys, had become world-famous. His reception was most brilliant. Dinner parties, receptions, invitations without end, attested the enthusiasm of the sober English; and his appearance at concerts and public meetings was the signal for stormy applause. How, in the press of all this pleasure in which he was plunged, he continued to compose the great number of works produced at this time, is a marvel. He must have been little less than a Briareus. It was in England that he wrote the celebrated Salomon symphonies, the "twelve grand," as they are called. They may well be regarded as the crowning-point of Haydn's efforts in that form of writing. He took infinite pains with them, as, indeed, is well proved by an examination of the scores. More elaborate, more beautiful, and scored for a fuller orchestra than any others of the one hundred and twenty or thereabouts which he composed, the Salomon set also bears marks of the devout and pious spirit in which Haydn ever labored.

It is interesting to see how, in many of the great works which have won the world's admiration, the religion of the author has gone hand in hand with his energy and his genius; and we find Haydn not ashamed to indorse his score with his prayer and praise, or to offer the fruits of his talents to the Giver of all. Thus, the symphony in D (No. 6) bears on the first page of the score the inscription, "In nomine Domini: di me Giuseppe Haydn, maia 1791, in London;" and on the last page, "Fine, Laus Deo, 238."

That genius may sometimes be trusted to judge of its own work may be gathered from Haydn's own estimate of these great symphonies.

"Sir," said the well-satisfied Salomon, after a successful performance of one of them, "I am strongly of opinion that you will never surpass these symphonies."
"No!" replied Haydn; "I never mean to try."
The public, as we have said, was enthusiastic; but such a full banquet of severe orchestral music was a severe trial to many, and not a few heads would keep time to the music by steady nods during the slow movements. Haydn, therefore, composed what is known as the "Surprise" symphony. The slow movement is of the most lulling and soothing character, and about the time the audience should be falling into its first snooze, the instruments having all died away into the softest *pianissimo*, the full orchestra breaks out with a frightful BANG. It is a question whether the most vigorous performance of this symphony would startle an audience nowadays, accustomed to the strident effects of Wagner and Liszt. A wag in a recent London journal tells us, indeed, that at the most critical part in the work a gentleman opened one eye sleepily and said, "Come in."

Simple-hearted Haydn was delighted at the attention lavished on him in London. He tells us how he enjoyed his various entertainments and feastings by such dignitaries as William Pitt, the Lord Chancellor, and the Duke of Lids (Leeds). The gentlemen drank freely the whole night, and the songs, the crazy uproar, and smashing of glasses were very great. He went down to stay with the Prince of Wales (George IV.) who played on the violoncello, and charmed the composer by his kindness. "He is the handsomest man on God's earth. He has an extraordinary love of music, and a great deal of feeling, but very little money."

To stem the tide of Haydn's popularity, the Italian faction had recourse to Giardini; and they even imported a pet pupil of Haydn, Pleyel, to conduct the rival concerts. Our composer kept his temper, and wrote: "He [Pleyel] behaves himself with great modesty." Later we read, "Pleyel's presumption is a public laughingstock;" but he adds, "I go to all his concerts and applaud him."

Far different were the amenities that passed between Haydn and Giardini. "I won't know the German hound," says the latter. Haydn wrote, "I attended his concert at Ranelagh, and he played the fiddle like a hog."

Among the pleasant surprises Haydn had in England was his visit to Herschel, the great astronomer, in whom he recognized one of his old oboe-players. The big telescope amazed him, and so did the patient star-gazer, who often sat out-of-doors in the most intense cold for five or six hours at a time.

Our composer returned to Vienna in May, 1795. with the little fortune of 12,000 florins in his pocket.

V.

In his charming little cottage near Vienna Haydn was the centre of a brilliant society. Princes and nobles were proud to do honor to him; and painters, poets, scholars, and musicians made a delightful coterie, which was not even disturbed by the political convulsions of the time. The baleful star of Napoleon shot its disturbing influences throughout Europe, and the roar of his cannon shook the established order of things with the echoes of what was to come. Haydn was passionately attached to his country and his emperor, and regarded anxiously the rumblings and quakings of the period; but he did not intermit his labor, or allow his consecration to his divine art to be in the least shaken. Like Archimedes of old, he toiled serenely at his appointed work, while the political order of things was crumbling before the genius and energy of the Corsican adventurer.

In 1798 he completed his great oratorio of "The Creation," on which he had spent three years of toil, and which embodied his brightest genius. Haydn was usually a very rapid composer, but he seems to have labored at the "Creation" with a sort of reverential humility, which never permitted him to think his work worthy or complete. It soon went the round of Germany, and passed to England and France, everywhere awakening enthusiasm by its great symmetry and beauty. Without the sublimity of Handel's "Messiah," it is marked by a richness of melody, a serene elevation, a matchless variety in treatment, which make it the most characteristic of Haydn's works. Napoleon, the first consul, was hastening to the opera-house to hear this, January 24, 1801, when he was stopped by an attempt at assassination.

Two years after "The Creation" appeared "The Seasons," founded on Thomson's poem, also a great work, and one of his last; for the grand old man was beginning to think of rest, and he only composed two or three quartets after this. He was now seventy years old, and went but little from his own home. His chief pleasure was to sit in his shady garden, and see his friends, who loved to solace the musical patriarch with cheerful talk and music. Haydn often fell into deep melancholy, and he tells us that God revived him; for no more sweet, devout nature ever lived. His art was ever a religion. A touching incident of his old age occurred at a grand performance of "The Creation" in 1808. Haydn was present, but he was so old and feeble that he had to be wheeled in a chair into the theatre, where a princess of the house of Ester-hazy took her seat by his side. This was the last time that Haydn appeared in public, and a very impressive sight it must have been to see the aged father of music listening to "The Creation" of his younger days, but too old to take any active share in the performance. The presence of the old man roused intense enthusiasm among the audience, which could no longer be suppressed as the chorus and orchestra burst in full power upon the superb passage, "And there was light."

Amid the tumult of the enraptured audience the old composer was seen striving to raise himself. Once on his feet, he mustered up all his strength, and, in reply to the applause of the audience, he cried out as loud as he was able: "No, no! not from me, but," pointing to heaven, "from thence—from heaven above—comes all!" saying which, he fell back in his chair, faint and exhausted, and had to be carried out of the room.

One year after this Vienna was bombarded by the French, and a shot fell in Haydn's garden. He requested to be led to his piano, and played the "Hymn to the Emperor" three times over with passionate eloquence and pathos. This was his last performance. He died five days afterward, aged seventy-seven, and lies buried in the cemetery of Gumpfenzdorf, in his own beloved Vienna.

VI.

The serene, genial face of Haydn, as seen in his portraits, measures accurately the character of his music. In both we see health fulness, good-humor, vivacity, devotional feeling, and warm affections; a mind contented, but yet attaching high importance to only one thing in life, the composing of music. Haydn pursued this with a calm, insatiable industry, without haste, without rest. His works number eight hundred, comprising cantatas, symphonies, oratorios, masses, concertos, trios, sonatas, quartets, minuets, etc., and also twenty-two operas, eight German and fourteen Italian.

As a creative mind in music, Haydn was the father of the quartet and symphony. Adopting the sonata form as scientifically illustrated by Emanuel Bach, he introduced it into compositions for the orchestra and the chamber. He developed these into a completeness and full-orbed symmetry, which have never been improved. Mozart is richer, Beethoven more sublime, Schubert more luxuriant, Mendelssohn more orchestral and passionate; but Haydn has never been surpassed in his keen perception of the capacities of instruments, his subtile distribution of parts, his variety in treating his themes, and his charmingly legitimate effects. He fills a large space in musical history, not merely from the number, originality, and beauty of his compositions, but as one who represents an era in art-development.

In Haydn genius and industry were happily united. With a marvelously rich flow of musical ideas, he clearly knew what he meant to do, and never neglected the just elaboration of each one. He would labor on a theme till it had shaped itself into perfect beauty.

Haydn is illustrious in the history of art as a complete artistic life, which worked out all of its contents as did the great Goethe. In the words of a charming writer: "His life was a rounded whole. There was no broken light about it; it orbed slowly, with a mild, unclouded lustre, into a perfect star. Time was gentle with him, and Death was kind, for both waited upon his genius until all was won. Mozart was taken away at an age when new and dazzling effects had not ceased to flash through his brain: at the very moment when his harmonies began to have a prophetic ring of the nineteenth century, it was decreed that he should not see its dawn. Beethoven himself had but just entered upon an unknown 'sea whose margin seemed to fade forever and forever as he moved;' but good old Haydn had come into port over a calm sea and after a prosperous voyage. The laurel wreath was this time woven about silver locks; the gathered-in harvest was ripe and golden."

MOZART.
I.

The life of Wolfgang Amadeus Mozart, one of the immortal names in music, contradicts the rule that extraordinary youthful talent is apt to be followed by a sluggish and commonplace maturity. His father entered the room one day with a friend, and found the child bending over a music score. The little Mozart, not yet five years old, told his father he was writing a concerto for the piano. The latter examined it, and tears of joy and astonishment rolled down his face on perceiving its accuracy.

"It is good, but too difficult for general use," said the friend.

"Oh," said Wolfgang, "it must be practised till it is learned. This is the way it goes." So saying, he played it with perfect correctness.

About the same time he offered to take the violin at a performance of some chamber music. His father refused, saying, "How can you? You have never learned the violin."

"One needs not study for that," said this musical prodigy; and taking the instrument, he played second violin with ease and accuracy. Such precocity seems almost incredible, and only in the history of music does it find any parallel.

Born in Salzburg, January 27, 1756, he was carefully trained by his father, who resigned his place as court musician to devote himself more exclusively to his family. From the earliest age he showed an extraordinary passion for music and mathematics, scrawling notes and diagrams in every place accessible to his insatiate pencil.

Taken to Vienna, the six-year-old virtuoso astonished the court by his brilliant talents. The future Queen of France, Marie Antoinette, was particularly delighted with him, and the little Mozart naively said he would like to marry her, for she was so good to him. His father devoted several years to an artistic tour, with him and his little less talented sister, through the German cities, and it was also extended to Paris and London. Everywhere the greatest enthusiasm was evinced in this charming bud of promise. The father writes home: "We have swords, laces, mantillas, snuff-boxes, gold cases, sufficient to furnish a shop; but as for money, it is a scarce article, and I am positively poor."

At Paris they were warmly received at the court, and the boy is said to have expressed his surprise when Mme. Pompadour refused to kiss him, saying: "Who is she, that she will not kiss me? Have I not been kissed by the queen?" In London his improvisations and piano sonatas excited the greatest admiration. Here he also published his third work. These journeys were an uninterrupted chain of triumphs for the child-virtuoso on the piano, organ, violin, and in singing. He was made honorary member of the Academies of Bologna and Verona, decorated with orders, and received at the age of thirteen an order to write the opera of "Mithridates," which was successfully produced at Milan in 1770. Several other fine minor compositions were also written to order at this time for his Italian admirers. At Rome Mozart attended the Sistine Chapel and wrote the score of Allegri's great mass, forbidden by the pope to be copied, from the memory of a single performance.

The record of Mozart's youthful triumphs might be extended at great length; but aside from the proof they furnish of his extraordinary precocity, they have lent little vital significance in the great problem of his career, except so far as they stimulated the marvelous boy to lay a deep foundation for his greater future, which, short as it was, was fruitful in undying results.

II.

Mozart's life in Paris, where he lived with his mother in 1778 and 1779, was a disappointment, for he despised the French nation. His deep, simple, German nature revolted from Parisian frivolity, in which he found only sensuality and coarseness, disguised under a thin veneering of social grace. He abhorred French music in these bitter terms: "The French are and always will be downright donkeys. They cannot sing, they scream." It was just at this time that Gluck and Piccini were having their great art-duel. We get a glimpse of the pious tendency of the young composer in his characterization of Voltaire: "The ungodly arch-villain, Voltaire, has just died like a dog." Again he writes: "Friends who have no religion cannot long be my friends.... I have such a sense of religion that I shall never do anything that I would not do before the whole world."

With Mozart's return to Germany in 1779, being then twenty-three years of age, comes the dawn of his classical period as a composer. The greater number of his masses had already been written, and now he settled himself in serious earnest to the cultivation of a true German operatic school. This found its dawn in the production of "Idomeneo," his first really great work for the lyric stage.

The young composer had hard struggles with poverty in these days. His letters to his father are full of revelations of his friction with the little worries of life. Lack of money pinched him close, yet his cheerful spirit was ever buoyant. "I have only one small room; it is quite crammed with a piano, a table, a bed, and a chest of drawers," he writes.

Yet he would marry; for he was willing to face poverty in the companionship of a loving woman who dared to face it with him. At Mannheim he had met a beautiful young singer, Aloysia Weber, and he went to Munich to offer her marriage. She, however, saw nothing attractive in the thin, pale young man, with his long nose, great eyes, and little head; for he was anything but prepossessing. A younger sister, Constance, however, secretly loved Mozart, and he soon transferred his repelled affections to this charming woman, whom he married in 1782 at the house of Baroness Waldstetten. His *naïve* reasons for marrying show Mozart's ingenuous nature. He had no one to take care of his linen, he would not live dissolutely like other young men, and he loved Constance Weber. His answer to his father, who objected on account of his poverty, is worth quoting:

"Constance is a well-conducted, good girl, of respectable parentage, and I am in a position to earn at least *daily bread* for her. We love each other, and are resolved to marry. All that you have written or may possibly write on the subject can be nothing but well-meant advice, which, however good and sensible, can no longer apply to a man who has gone so far with a girl."

Poor as Mozart was, he possessed such integrity and independence that he refused a most liberal offer from the King of Prussia to become his chapel-master, for some unexplained reason which involved his sense of right and wrong. The first year of his marriage he wrote "Il Seraglio," and made the acquaintance of the aged Gluck, who took a deep interest in him and warmly praised his genius. Haydn, too, recognized his brilliant powers. "I tell you, on the word of an honest man," said the author of the "Creation" to Leopold Mozart, the father, who asked his opinion, "that I consider your son the greatest composer I have ever heard. He writes with taste, and possesses a thorough knowledge of composition."

Poverty and increasing expense pricked Mozart into intense, restless energy. His life had no lull in its creative industry. His splendid genius, insatiable and tireless, broke down his body, like a sword wearing out its scabbard. He poured out symphonies, operas, and sonatas with such prodigality as to astonish us, even when recollecting how fecund the musical mind has often been. Alike as artist and composer, he never ceased his labors. Day after day and night after night he hardly snatched an hour's rest. We can almost fancy he foreboded how short his brilliant life was to be, and was impelled to crowd into its brief compass its largest measure of results.

Yet he was always pursued by the spectre of want. Oftentimes his sick wife could not obtain needed medicines. He made more money than most musicians, yet was always impoverished. But it was his glory that he was never impoverished by sensual indulgence, extravagance, and riotous living, but by his lavish generosity to those who in many instances needed help less than himself. Like many other men of genius and sensibility, he could not say "no" to even the pretense of distress and suffering.

III.

The culminating point of Mozart's artistic development was in 1786. The "Marriage of Figaro" was the first of a series of masterpieces which cannot be surpassed alike for musical greatness and their hold on the lyric stage. The next year "Don Giovanni" saw the light, and was produced at Prague. The overture of this opera was composed and scored in less than six hours. The inhabitants of Prague greeted the work with the wildest enthusiasm, for they seemed to understand Mozart better than the Viennese.

During this period he made frequent concert tours to recruit his fortunes, but with little financial success. Presents of watches, snuff-boxes, and rings were common, but the returns were so small that Mozart was frequently obliged to pawn his gifts to purchase a dinner and lodging. What a comment on the period which adored genius, but allowed it to starve! His audiences could be enthusiastic enough to carry him to his hotel on their shoulders, but probably never thought that the wherewithal of a hearty supper was a more seasonable homage. So our musician struggled on through the closing years of his life with the wolf constantly at his door, and an invalid wife whom he passionately loved, yet must needs see suffer from the want of common necessaries. In these modern days, when distinguished artists make princely fortunes by the exercise of their musical gifts, it is not easy to believe that Mozart, recognized as the greatest pianoforte player and composer of his time by all of musical Germany, could suffer such dire extremes of want as to be obliged more than once to beg for a dinner. In

1791 he composed the score of the "Magic Flute" at the request of Schikaneder, a Viennese manager, who had written the text from a fairy tale, the fantastic elements of which are peculiarly German in their humor. Mozart put great earnestness into the work, and made it the first German opera of commanding merit, which embodied the essential intellectual sentiment and kindly warmth of popular German life. The manager paid the composer but a trifle for a work whose transcendent success enabled him to build a new opera-house and laid the foundation of a large fortune. We are told, too, that at the time of Mozart's death in extreme want, when his sick wife, half maddened with grief, could not buy a coffin for the dead composer, this hard-hearted wretch, who owed his all to the genius of the great departed, rushed about through Vienna bewailing the loss to music with sentimental tears, but did not give the heart-broken widow one kreutzer to pay the expense of a decent burial.

In 1791 Mozart's health was breaking down with great rapidity, though he himself would never recognize his own swiftly advancing fate. He experienced, however, a deep melancholy which nothing could remove. For the first time his habitual cheerfulness deserted him. His wife had been enabled through the kindness of her friends to visit the healing waters of Baden, and was absent.

An incident now occurred which impressed Mozart with an ominous chill. One night there came a stranger, singularly dressed in gray, with an order for a requiem to be composed without fail within a month. The visitor, without revealing his name, departed in mysterious gloom, as he came. Again the stranger called and solemnly reminded Mozart of his promise. The composer easily persuaded himself that this was a visitor from the other world, and that the requiem would be his own; for he was exhausted with labor and sickness, and easily became the prey of superstitious fancies. When his wife returned, she found him with a fatal pallor on his face, silent and melancholy, laboring with intense absorption on the funereal mass. He would sit brooding over the score till he swooned away in his chair, and only come to consciousness to bend his waning energies again to their ghastly work. The mysterious visitor, whom Mozart believed to be the precursor of his death, we now know to have been Count Walseck, who had recently lost his wife, and wished a musical memorial.

His final sickness attacked the composer while laboring at the requiem. The musical world was ringing with the fame of his last opera. To the dying man was brought the offer of the rich appointment of organist of St. Stephen's Cathedral. Most flattering propositions were made him by eager managers, who had become thoroughly awake to his genius when it was too late. The great Mozart was dying in the very prime of his youth and his powers, when success was in his grasp and the world opening wide its arms to welcome his glorious gifts with substantial recognition; but all too late; for he was doomed to die in his spring-tide, though "a spring mellow with all the fruits of autumn."

The unfinished requiem lay on the bed, and his last efforts were to imitate some peculiar instrumental effects, as he breathed out his life in the arms of his wife and his friend Süssmaier.

The epilogue to this life-drama is one of the saddest in the history of art: a pauper funeral for one of the world's greatest geniuses. "It was late one winter afternoon," says an old record, "before the coffin was deposited on the side aisles on the south side of St. Stephen's. Van Swieten, Salieri, Süssmaier, and two unknown musicians were the only persons present besides the officiating priest and the pall-bearers. It was a terribly inclement day; rain and sleet came down fast; and an eye-witness describes how the little band of mourners stood shivering in the blast, with their umbrellas up, round the hearse, as it left the door of the church. It was then far on in the dark cold December afternoon, and the evening was fast closing in before the solitary hearse had passed the Stubenthor, and reached the distant graveyard of St. Marx, in which, among the 'third class,' the great composer of the 'G minor Symphony' and the 'Requiem' found his resting-place. By this time the weather had proved too much for all the mourners; they had dropped off one by one, and Mozart's body was accompanied only by the driver of the carriage. There had been already two pauper funerals that day—one of them a midwife—and Mozart was to be the third in the grave and the uppermost.

"When the hearse drew up in the slush and sleet at the gate of the graveyard, it was welcomed by a strange pair, Franz Harruschka, the assistant grave-digger, and his mother Katharina, known as 'Frau Katha,' who filled the quaint office of official mendicant to the place.

"The old woman was the first to speak: 'Any coaches or mourners coming?'

"A shrug from the driver of the hearse was the only response.

"'Whom have you got there, then?' continued she.

"'A band-master,' replied the other.

"'A musician? they're a poor lot; then I've no more money to look for to-day. It is to be hoped we shall have better luck in the morning.'

"To which the driver said, with a laugh: 'I'm devilish thirsty, too—not a kreutzer of drink-money have I had.'

"After this curious colloquy the coffin was dismounted and shoved into the top of the grave already occupied by the two paupers of the morning; and such was Mozart's last appearance on earth."

To-day no stone marks the spot where were deposited the last remains of one of the brightest of musical spirits; indeed, the very grave is unknown, for it was the grave of a pauper.

IV.

Mozart's charming letters reveal to us such a gentle, sparkling, affectionate nature, as to inspire as much love for the man as admiration for his genius. Sunny humor and tenderness bubble in almost every sentence. A clever writer says that "opening these is like opening a painted tomb.... The colors are all fresh, the figures are all distinct."

No better illustration of the man Mozart can be had than in a few extracts from his correspondence.

He writes to his sister from Rome while yet a mere lad:

"I am, thank God! except my miserable pen, well, and send you and mamma a thousand kisses. I wish you were in Rome; I am sure it would please you. Papa says I am a little fool, but that is nothing new. Here we have but one bed; it is easy to understand that I can't rest comfortably with papa. I shall be glad when we get into new quarters. I have just finished drawing the Holy Peter with his keys, the Holy Paul with his sword, and the Holy Luke with my sister. I have had the honor of kissing St. Peter's foot; and because I am so small as to be unable to reach it, they had to lift me up. I am the same old "Wolfgang."

Mozart was very fond of this sister Nannerl, and he used to write to her in a playful mosaic of French, German, and Italian. Just after his wedding he writes:

"My darling is now a hundred times more joyful at the idea of going to Salzburg, and I am willing to stake—ay, my very life, that you will rejoice still more in my happiness when you know her; if, indeed, in your estimation, as in mine, a high-principled, honest, virtuous, and pleasing wife ought to make a man happy."

Late in his short life he writes the following characteristic note to a friend, whose life does not appear to have been one of the most regular:

"Now tell me, my dear friend, how you are. I hope you are all as well as we are. You cannot fail to be happy, for you possess everything that you can wish for at your age and in your position, especially as you now seem to have entirely given up your former mode of life. Do you not every day become more convinced of the truth of the little lectures I used to inflict on you? Are not the pleasures of a transient, capricious passion widely different from the happiness produced by rational and true love? I feel sure that you often in your heart thank me for my admonitions. I shall feel quite proud if you do. But, jesting apart, you do really owe me some little gratitude if you are become worthy of Fräulein N———, for I certainly played no insignificant part in your improvement or reform.

"My great-grandfather used to say to his wife, my great-grandmother, who in turn told it to her daughter, my mother, who repeated it to her daughter, my own sister, that it was a very great art to talk eloquently and well, but an equally great one to know the right moment to stop. I therefore shall follow the advice of my sister, thanks to our mother, grandmother, and great-grandmother, and thus end, not only my moral ebullition, but my letter."

His playful tenderness lavished itself on his wife in a thousand quaint ways. He would, for example, rise long before her to take his horseback exercise, and always kiss her sleeping face and leave a little note like the following resting on her forehead: "Good-morning, dear little wife! I hope you have had a good sleep and pleasant dreams. I shall be back in two hours. Behave yourself like a good little girl, and don't run away from your husband."

Speaking of an infant child, our composer would say merrily, "That boy will be a true Mozart, for he always cries in the very key in which I am playing."

Mozart's musical greatness, shown in the symmetry of his art as well as in the richness of his inspirations, has been unanimously acknowledged by his brother composers. Meyerbeer could not restrain his tears when speaking of him. Weber,

Mendelssohn, Rossini, and Wagner always praise him in terms of enthusiastic admiration. Haydn called him the greatest of composers. In fertility of invention, beauty of form, and exactness of method, he has never been surpassed, and has but one or two rivals. The composer of three of the greatest operas in musical history, besides many of much more than ordinary excellence; of symphonies that rival Haydn's for symmetry and melodic affluence; of a great number of quartets, quintets, etc.; and of pianoforte sonatas which rank high among the best; of many masses that are standard in the service of the Catholic Church; of a great variety of beautiful songs—there is hardly any form of music which he did not richly adorn with the treasures of his genius. We may well say, in the words of one of his most competent critics:

"Mozart was a king and a slave—king in his own beautiful realm of music; slave of the circumstances and the conditions of this world. Once over the boundaries of his own kingdom, and he was supreme; but the powers of the earth acknowledged not his sovereignty."

BEETHOVEN.

I.

The name and memory of this composer awaken, in the heart of the lover of music, sentiments of the deepest reverence and admiration. His life was so marked with affliction and so isolated as to make him, in his environment of conditions as a composer, a unique figure.

The principal fact which made the exterior life of Beethoven so bare of the ordinary pleasures that brighten and sweeten existence, his total deafness, greatly enriched his spiritual life. Music finally became to him a purely intellectual conception, for he was without any sensual enjoyment of its effects. To this Samson of music, for whom the ear was like the eye to other men, Milton's lines may indeed well apply:

"Oh! dark, dark, dark, amid the blaze of noon!
Irrecoverably dark—total eclipse,
Without all hope of day!
Oh first created Beam, and thou, great Word,
'Let there be light,' and light was over all,
Why am I thus bereaved thy prime decree?
The sun to me is dark."

To his severe affliction we owe alike many of the defects of his character and the splendors of his genius. All his powers, concentrated into a spiritual focus, wrought such things as lift him into a solitary greatness. The world has agreed to measure this man as it measures Homer, Dante, and Shakespeare. We do not compare him with others.

Beethoven had the reputation among his contemporaries of being harsh, bitter, suspicious, and unamiable. There is much to justify this in the circumstances of his life; yet our readers will discover much to show, on the other hand, how deep, strong, and tender was the heart which was so wrung and tortured, and wounded to the quick by—

"The slings and arrows of outrageous fortune."

Weber gives a picture of Beethoven: "The square Cyclopean figure attired in a shabby coat with torn sleeves." Everybody will remember his noble, austere face, as seen in the numerous prints: the square, massive head, with the forest of rough hair; the strong features, so furrowed with the marks of passion and sadness; the eyes, with their look of introspection and insight; the whole expression of the countenance as of an ancient prophet. Such was the impression made by Beethoven on all who saw him, except in his moods of fierce wrath, which toward the last were not uncommon, though short-lived. A sorely tried, sublimely gifted man, he met his fate stubbornly, and worked out his great mission with all his might and main, through long years of weariness and trouble. Posterity has rewarded him by enthroning him on the highest peaks of musical fame.

II.

Ludwig van Beethoven was born at Bonn, in 1770. It is a singular fact that at an early age he showed the deepest distaste for music, unlike the other great composers, who evinced their bent from their earliest years. His father was obliged to whip him severely before he would consent to sit down at the harpsichord; and it was not till he was past ten that his genuine interest in music showed itself. His first compositions displayed his genius. Mozart heard him play them, and said, "Mind, you will hear that boy talked of." Haydn, too, met Beethoven for the first and only time when the former was on his way to England, and recognized his remarkable powers. He gave him a few lessons in composition, and was after that anxious to claim the young Titan as a pupil.

"Yes," growled Beethoven, who for some queer reason never liked Haydn, "I had some lessons of him, indeed, but I was not his disciple. I never learned anything from him."

Beethoven made a profound impression even as a youth on all who knew him. Aside from the palpable marks of his power, there was an indomitable *hauteur*, a mysterious, self-wrapped air as of one constantly communing with the invisible, an unconscious assertion of mastery about him, which strongly impressed the imagination.

At the very outset of his career, when life promised all fair and bright things to him, two comrades linked themselves to him, and ever after that refused to give him up—grim poverty and still grimmer disease. About the same time that he lost a fixed salary through the death of his friend the Elector of Cologne, he began to grow deaf. Early in 1800, walking one day in the woods with his devoted friend and pupil, Ferdinand Ries, he disclosed the sad secret to him that the whole joyous world of sound was being gradually closed up to him; the charm of the human voice, the notes of the woodland birds, the sweet babblings of Nature, jargon to others, but intelligible to genius, the full-born splendors of *heard* music —all, all were fast receding from his grasp.

Beethoven was extraordinarily sensitive to the influences of Nature. Before his disease became serious he writes: "I wander about here with music-paper among the hills, and dales, and valleys, and scribble a good deal. No man on earth can love the country as I do." But one of Nature's most delightful modes of speech to man was soon to be utterly lost to him. At last he became so deaf that the most stunning crash of thunder or the *fortissimo* of the full orchestra were to him as if they were not. His bitter, heartrending cry of agony, when he became convinced that the misfortune was irremediable, is full of eloquent despair: "As autumn leaves wither and fall, so are my hopes blighted. Almost as I came, I depart. Even the lofty courage, which so often animated me in the lovely days of summer, is gone forever. O Providence! vouchsafe me one day of pure felicity! How long have I been estranged from the glad echo of true joy! When, O my God! when shall I feel it again in the temple of Nature and man? Never!"

And the small-souled, mole-eyed gossips and critics called him hard, churlish, and cynical—him, for whom the richest thing in Nature's splendid dower had been obliterated, except a soul, which never in its deepest sufferings lost its noble faith in God and man, or allowed its indomitable courage to be one whit weakened. That there were periods of utterly rayless despair and gloom we may guess; but not for long did Beethoven's great nature cower before its evil genius.

III.

Within three years, from 1805 to 1808, Beethoven composed some of his greatest works: the oratorio of "The Mount of Olives," the opera of "Fidelio," and the two noble symphonies, "Pastorale" and "Eroica," besides a large number of concertos, sonatas, songs, and other occasional pieces. However gloomy the externals of his life, his creative activities knew no cessation.

The "Sinfonia Eroica," the "Choral" only excepted, is the longest of the immortal nine, and is one of the greatest examples of musical portraiture extant. All the great composers from Handel to Wagner have attempted what is called descriptive music with more or less success, but never have musical genius and skill achieved a result so admirable in its relation to its purpose and by such strictly legitimate means as in this work.

"The 'Eroica,'" says a great writer, "is an attempt to draw a musical portrait of an historical character—a great statesman, a great general, a noble individual; to represent in music—Beethoven's own language—what M. Thiers has given in words and Paul Delaroche in painting." Of Beethoven's success another writer has said: "It wants no title to tell its meaning, for throughout the symphony the hero is visibly portrayed."

It is anything but difficult to realize why Beethoven should have admired the first Napoleon. Both the soldier and musician were made of that sturdy stuff which would and did defy the world; and it is not strange that Beethoven should have desired in some way—and he knew of no better course than through his art—to honor one so characteristically akin to himself, and who at that time was the most prominent man in Europe. Beethoven began the work in 1802, and in 1804 it was completed, and bore the following title:

Sinfonia grande

"Napoleon Bonaparte"

1804 in August

del Sigr

Louis van Beethoven

Sinfonia 3.

Op. 55.

This was copied and the original score dispatched to the embassador for presentation, while Beethoven retained the copy. Before the composition was laid before Napoleon, however, the great general had accepted the title of Emperor. No sooner did Beethoven hear of this from his pupil Ries than he started up in a rage, and exclaimed: "After all, then, he's nothing but an ordinary mortal! He will trample the rights of men under his feet!" saying which, he rushed to his table, seized the copy of the score, and tore the title-page completely off. From this time Beethoven hated Napoleon, and never again spoke of him in connection with the symphony until he heard of his death in St. Helena, when he observed, "I have already composed music for this calamity," evidently referring to the "Funeral March" in this symphony.

The opera of "Fidelio," which he composed about the same time, may be considered, in the severe sense of a great and symmetrical musical work, the finest lyric drama ever written, with the possible exception of Gluck's "Orpheus and Eurydice" and "Iphigenia in Tauris." It is rarely performed, because its broad, massive, and noble effects are beyond the capacity of most singers, and belong to the domain of pure music, demanding but little alliance with the artistic clap-trap of startling scenery and histrionic extravagance. Yet our composer's conscience shows its completeness in his obedience to the law of opera; for the music he has written to express the situations cannot be surpassed for beauty, pathos, and passion. Beethoven, like Mendelssohn, revolted from the idea of lyric drama as an art-inconsistency, but he wrote "Fidelio" to show his possibilities in a direction with which he had but little sympathy.

He composed four overtures for this opera at different periods, on account of the critical caprices of the Viennese public—a concession to public taste which his stern independence rarely made.

IV.

Beethoven's relations with women were peculiar and characteristic, as were all the phases of a nature singularly self-poised and robust. Like all men of powerful imagination and keen (though perhaps not delicate) sensibility, he was strongly attracted toward the softer sex. But a certain austerity of morals, and that purity of feeling which is the inseparable shadow of one's devotion to lofty aims, always kept him within the bounds of Platonic affection. Yet there is enough in Beethoven's letters, as scanty as their indications are in this direction, to show what ardor and glow of feeling he possessed.

About the time that he was suffering keenly with the knowledge of his fast-growing infirmity, he was bound by a strong tie of affection to Countess Giulietta Guicciardi, his "immortal beloved," "his angel," "his all," "his life," as he called her in a variety of passionate utterances. It was to her that he dedicated his song "Adelaida," which as an expression of lofty passion is world-famous. Beethoven was very much dissatisfied with the work even in the glow of composition. Before the notes were dry on the music paper, the composer's old friend Barth was announced. "Here," said Beethoven, putting a roll of score paper in Earth's hands, "look at that. I have just finished it, and don't like it. There is hardly fire enough in the stove to burn it, but I will try." Barth glanced through the composition, then sang it, and soon grew into such enthusiasm as to draw from Beethoven the expression, "No? then we will not burn it, old fellow." Whether it was the reaction of disgust, which so often comes to genius after the tension of work, or whether his ideal of its lovely theme was so high as to make all effort seem inadequate, the world came very near losing what it could not afford to have missed.

The charming countess, however, preferred rank, wealth, and unruffled ease to being linked even with a great genius, if, indeed, the affair ever looked in the direction of marriage. She married another, and Beethoven does not seem to have been seriously disturbed. It may be that, like Goethe, he valued the love of woman not for itself or its direct results, but as an art-stimulus which should enrich and fructify his own intellectual life.

We get glimpses of successors to the fair countess. The beautiful Marie Pachler was for some time the object of his adoration. The affair is a somewhat mysterious one, and the lady seems to have suffered from the fire through which her powerful companion passed unscathed. Again, quaintest and oddest of all, is the fancy kindled by that "mysterious sprite of genius," as one of her contemporaries calls her, Bettina Brentano, the gifted child-woman, who fascinated all who came within her reach, from Goethe and Beethoven down to princes and nobles. Goethe's correspondence with this strange being has embalmed her life in classic literature.

Our composer's intercourse with women—for he was always alive to the charms of female society—was for the most part homely and practical in the extreme, after his deafness destroyed the zest of the more romantic phases of the divine passion. He accepted adoration, as did Dean Swift, as a right. He permitted his female admirers to knit him stockings and comforters, and make him dainty puddings and other delicacies, which he devoured with huge gusto. He condescended, in return, to go to sleep on their sofas, after picking his teeth with the candle-snuffers (so says scandal), while they thrummed away at his sonatas, the artistic slaughter of which Beethoven was mercifully unable to hear.

V.

The friendship of the Archduke Rudolph relieved Beethoven of the immediate pressure of poverty; for in 1809 he settled a small life-pension upon him. The next ten years were passed by him in comparative ease and comfort, and in this time he gave to the world five of his immortal symphonies, and a large number of his finest sonatas and masses. His general health improved very much; and in his love for his nephew Karl, whom Beethoven had adopted, the lonely man found an outlet for his strong affections, which was medicine for his soul, though the object was worthless and ungrateful.

We get curious and amusing insights into the daily tenor of Beethoven's life during this period—things sometimes almost grotesque, were they not so sad. The composer lived a solitary life, and was very much at the mercy of his servants on account of his self-absorption and deafness. He was much worried by these prosaic cares. One story of a slatternly servant is as follows: The master was working at the mass in D, the great work which he commenced in 1819 for the celebration of the appointment of the Archduke Rudolph as Archbishop of Olmutz, and which should have been completed by the following year. Beethoven, however, became so engrossed with his work, and increased its proportions so much, that it was not finished until some two years after the event which it was intended to celebrate. While Beethoven was engaged upon this score, he one day woke up to the fact that some of his pages were missing. "Where on earth could they be?" he asked himself, and the servant too; but the problem remained unsolved. Beethoven, beside himself, spent hours and hours in searching, and so did the servant, but it was all in vain. At last they gave up the task as a useless one, and Beethoven, mad with despair, and pouring the very opposite to blessings upon the head of her who, he believed, was the author of the mischief, sat down with the conclusion that he must rewrite the missing part. He had no sooner commenced a new Kyrie—for this was the movement which was not to be found —than some loose sheets of score paper were discovered in the kitchen! Upon examination they proved to be the identical pages that Beethoven so much desired, and which the woman, in her anxiety to be "tidy" and to "keep things straight," had appropriated at some time or other for wrapping up, not only old boots and clothes, but also some superannuated pots and pans that were greasy and black!

Thus he was continually fretted by the carelessness or the rascality of the servants in whom he was obliged to trust. He writes in his diary: "Nancy is too uneducated for a housekeeper—indeed, quite a beast." "My precious servants were occupied from seven o'clock till ten trying to kindle a fire." "The cook's off again." "I shied half a dozen books at her head." They made his dinner so nasty he couldn't eat it. "No soup to-day, no beef, no eggs. Got something from the inn at last."

His temper and peculiarities, too, made it difficult for him to live in peace with landlords and fellow-lodgers. As his deafness increased, he struck and thumped harder at the keys of his piano, the sound of which he could scarcely hear. Nor was this all. The music that filled his brain gave him no rest. He became an inspired madman. For hours he would pace the room "howling and roaring" (as his pupil Ries puts it); or he would stand beating time with hand and foot to the music which was so vividly present to his mind. This soon put him into a feverish excitement, when, to cool himself, he would take his water-jug, and, thoughtless of everything, pour its contents over his hands, after which he could sit down to his piano. With all this it can easily be imagined that Beethoven was frequently remonstrated with. The landlord complained of a damaged ceiling, and the fellow-lodgers declared that either they or the madman must leave the house, for they could get no rest where he was. So Beethoven never for long had a resting-place. Impatient at being interfered with, he immediately packed up and went off to some other vacant lodging. From this cause he was at one time paying the rent of four lodgings at once. At times he would get tired of this changing from one place to another—from the suburbs to the town—and then he would fall back upon the hospitable home of a patron, once again taking possession of an apartment which he had vacated, probably without the least explanation or cause. One admirer of his genius, who always reserved him a chamber in his establishment, used to say to his servants: "Leave it empty; Beethoven is sure to come back again."

The instant that Beethoven entered the house he began to write and cipher on the walls, the blinds, the table, everything, in the most abstracted manner. He frequently composed on slips of paper, which he afterward misplaced, so that he had great difficulty in finding them. At one time, indeed, he forgot his own name and the date of his birth.

It is said that he once went into a Viennese restaurant, and, instead of giving an order, began to write a score on the back of the bill-of-fare, absorbed and unconscious of time and place. At last he asked how much he owed. "You owe nothing, sir," said the waiter. "What! do you think I have not dined?" "Most assuredly." "Very well, then, give me something." "What do you wish?" "Anything."

These infirmities do not belittle the man of genius, but set off his greatness as with a foil. They illustrate the thought of Goethe: "It is all the same whether one is great or small, he has to pay the reckoning of humanity."

VI.

Yet beneath these eccentricities what wealth of tenderness, sympathy, and kindliness existed! His affection for his graceless nephew Karl is a touching picture. With the rest of his family he had never been on very cordial terms. His feeling of contempt for snobbery and pretense is very happily illustrated in his relations with his brother Johann. The latter had acquired property, and he sent Ludwig his card, inscribed "Johann van Beethoven, land-owner." The caustic reply was a card, on which was written, "Ludwig van Beethoven, brain-owner." But on Karl all the warmest feelings of a nature which had been starving to love and be loved poured themselves out. He gave the scapegrace every luxury and indulgence, and, self-absorbed as he was in an ideal sphere, felt the deepest interest in all the most trivial things that concerned him. Much to the uncle's sorrow, Karl cared nothing for music; but, worst of all, he was an idle, selfish, heartless fellow, who sneered at his benefactor, and valued him only for what he could get from him. At last Beethoven became fully aware of the lying ingratitude of his nephew, and he exclaims: "I know now you have no pleasure in coming to see me, which is only natural, for my atmosphere is too pure for you. God has never yet forsaken me, and no doubt some one will be found to close my eyes." Yet the generous old man forgave him, for he says in the codicil of his will, "I appoint my nephew Karl my sole heir."

Frequently, glimpses of the true vein showed themselves in such little episodes as that which occurred when Moscheles, accompanied by his brother, visited the great musician for the first time.

"Arrived at the door of the house," writes Moscheles, "I had some misgivings, knowing Beethoven's strong aversion to strangers. I therefore told my brother to wait below. After greeting Beethoven, I said: 'Will you permit me to introduce my brother to you?'

"'Where is he?' he suddenly replied.

"'Below.'

"'What, down-stairs?' and Beethoven immediately rushed off, seized hold of my brother, saying: 'Am I such a savage that you are afraid to come near me?'

"After this he showed great kindness to us."

While referring to the relations of Moscheles and Beethoven, the following anecdote related by Mme. Moscheles will be found suggestive. The pianist had been arranging some numbers of "Fidelio," which he took to the composer. He, *à la* Haydn, had inscribed the score with the words, "By God's help." Beethoven did not fail to perceive this, and he wrote underneath this phylactory the characteristic advice: "O man, help thyself."

The genial and sympathetic nature of Beethoven is illustrated in this quaint incident:

It was in the summer of 1811 that Ludwig Lowe, the actor, first met Beethoven in the dining-room of the Blue Star at Toplitz. Lowe was paying his addresses to the landlord's daughter; and conversation being impossible at the hour he dined there, the charming creature one day whispered to him: "Come at a later hour when the customers are gone and only Beethoven is here. He cannot hear, and will therefore not be in the way." This answered for a time; but the stern parents, observing the acquaintanceship, ordered the actor to leave the house and not to return. "How great was our despair!" relates Lowe. "We both desired to correspond, but through whom? Would the solitary man at the opposite table assist us? Despite his serious reserve and seeming churlishness, I believe he is not unfriendly. I have often caught a kind smile across his bold, defiant face." Lôwe determined to try. Knowing Beethoven's custom, he contrived to meet the master when he was walking in the gardens. Beethoven instantly recognized him, and asked the reason why he no longer dined at the Blue Star. A full confession was made, and then Lowe timidly asked if he would take charge of a letter to give to the girl.

"Why not?" pleasantly observed the rough-looking musician. "You mean what is right."

So pocketing the note, he was making his way onward when Lowe again interfered.

"I beg your pardon, Herr van Beethoven, that is not all."

"So, so," said the master.

"You must also bring back the answer," Lowe went on to say.

"Meet me here at this time to-morrow," said Beethoven.

Lowe did so, and there found Beethoven awaiting him, with the coveted reply from his lady-love. In this manner Beethoven carried the letters backward and forward for some five or six weeks—in short, as long as he remained in the town.

His friendship with Ferdinand Ries commenced in a way which testified how grateful he was for kindness. When his mother lay ill at Bonn, he hurried home from Vienna just in time to witness her death. After the funeral he suffered greatly from poverty, and was relieved by Ries the violinist. Years afterward young Ries waited on Beethoven with a letter of introduction from his father. The composer received him with cordial warmth, and said: "Tell your father I have not forgotten the death of my mother." Ever afterward he was a helpful and devoted friend to young Ries, and was of inestimable value in forwarding his musical career.

Beethoven in his poverty never forgot to be generous. At a concert given in aid of wounded soldiers, where he conducted, he indignantly refused payment with the words: "Say Beethoven never accepts anything where humanity is concerned." To an Ursuline convent he gave an entirely new symphony to be performed at their benefit concert. Friend or enemy never applied to him for help that he did not freely give, even to the pinching of his own comfort.

VII.

Rossini could write best when he was under the influence of Italian wine and sparkling champagne. Paesiello liked the warm bed in which to jot down his musical notions, and we are told that "it was between the sheets that he planned the 'Barber of Seville,' the 'Molinara,' and so many other *chefs-d'oeuvre* of ease and gracefulness." Mozart could chat and play at billiards or bowls at the same time that he composed the most beautiful music. Sacchini found it impossible to write anything of any beauty unless a pretty woman was by his side, and he was surrounded by his cats, whose graceful antics stimulated and affected him in a marked fashion. "Gluck," Bombet says, "in order to warm his imagination and to transport himself to Aulis or Sparta, was accustomed to place himself in the middle of a beautiful meadow. In this situation, with his piano before him, and a bottle of champagne on each side, he wrote in the open air his two 'Iphigenias,' his 'Orpheus,' and some other works." The agencies which stimulated Beethoven's grandest thoughts are eminently characteristic of the man. He loved to let the winds and storms beat on his bare head, and see the dazzling play of the lightning. Or, failing the sublimer moods of Nature, it was his delight to walk in the woods and fields, and take in at every pore the influences which she so lavishly bestows on her favorites. His true life was his ideal life in art. To him it was a mission and an inspiration, the end and object of all things; for these had value only as they fed the divine craving within.

"Nothing can be more sublime," he writes, "than to draw nearer to the Godhead than other men, and to diffuse here on earth these Godlike rays among mortals." Again: "What is all this compared to the grandest of all Masters of Harmony—above, above?"

"All experience seemed an arch, wherethrough
Gleamed that untraveled world, whose margin fades
Forever and forever as we move."

The last four years of our composer's life were passed amid great distress from poverty and feebleness. He could compose but little; and, though his friends solaced his latter days with attention and kindness, his sturdy independence would not accept more. It is a touching fact that Beethoven voluntarily suffered want and privation in his last years, that he might leave the more to his selfish and ungrateful nephew. He died in 1827, in his fifty-seventh year, and is buried in the Wahring Cemetery near Vienna. Let these extracts from a testamentary paper addressed to his brothers in 1802, in expectation of death, speak more eloquently of the hidden life of a heroic soul than any other words could:

"O ye, who consider or declare me to be hostile, obstinate, or misanthropic, what injustice ye do me! Ye know not the secret causes of that which to you wears such an appearance. My heart and my mind were from childhood prone to the tender feelings of affection. Nay, I was always disposed even to perform great actions. But, only consider that, for the last six years, I have been attacked by an incurable complaint, aggravated by the unskillful treatment of medical men, disappointed from year to year in the hope of relief, and at last obliged to submit to the endurance of an evil the cure of which may last perhaps for years, if it is practicable at all. Born with a lively, ardent disposition, susceptible to to the diversions of society, I was forced at an early age to renounce them, and to pass my life in seclusion. If I strove at any time to set myself above all this, oh how cruelly was I driven back by the doubly painful experience of my defective hearing! and yet it was not possible for me to say to people, 'Speak louder—bawl—for I am deaf!' Ah! how could I proclaim the defect of a sense that I once possessed in the highest perfection—in a perfection in which few of my colleagues possess or ever did possess it? Indeed, I cannot! Forgive me, then, if ye see me draw back when I would gladly mingle among you. Doubly mortifying is my misfortune to me, as it must tend to cause me to be misconceived. From recreation in the society of my fellow-creatures, from the pleasures of conversation, from the effusions of friendship, I am cut off. Almost alone in the world, I dare not venture into society more than absolute necessity requires. I am obliged to live as an exile. If I go into company, a painful anxiety comes over me, since I am apprehensive of being exposed to the danger of betraying my situation. Such has been my state, too, during this half year that I have spent in the country. Enjoined by my intelligent physician to spare my hearing as much as possible, I have been almost encouraged by him in my present natural disposition, though, hurried away by my fondness for society, I sometimes suffered myself to be enticed into it. But what a humiliation when any one standing beside me could hear at a distance a flute that I could not hear, or any one heard the shepherd singing, and I could not distinguish a sound! Such circumstances brought me to the brink of despair, and had well-nigh made me put an end to my life: nothing but my art held my hand. Ah! it seemed to me impossible to quit the world before I had produced all that I felt myself called to accomplish. And so I endured this wretched life—so truly wretched, that a somewhat speedy change is capable of transporting me from the best into the worst condition. Patience—so I am told—I must choose for my guide. Steadfast, I hope, will be my resolution to persevere, till it shall please the inexorable Fates to cut the thread. Perhaps there may be an amendment—perhaps not; I am prepared for the worst—I, who so early as my twenty-eighth year was forced to become a philosopher—it is not easy—for the artist more difficult than for any other. O God! thou lookest down upon my misery; thou knowest that it is accompanied with love of my fellow-creatures, and a disposition to do good! O men! when ye shall read this, think that ye have wronged me; and let the child of affliction take comfort on finding one like himself, who, in spite of all the impediments of Nature, yet did all that lay in his power to obtain admittance into the rank of worthy artists and men.... I go to meet death with joy. If he comes before I have had occasion to develop all my professional abilities, he will come too soon for me, in spite of my hard fate, and I should wish that he had delayed his arrival. But even then I am content, for he will release me from a state of endless suffering. Come when thou wilt, I shall meet thee with firmness. Farewell, and do not quite forget me after I am dead; I have deserved that you should think of me, for in my lifetime I have often thought of you to make you happy. May you ever be so!"

VIII.

The music of Beethoven has left a profound impress on art. In speaking of his genius it is difficult to keep expression within the limits of good taste. For who has so passed into the very inner *penetralia* of his great art, and revealed to the world such heights and depths of beauty and power in sound?

Beethoven composed nine symphonies, which, by one voice, are ranked as the greatest ever written, reaching in the last, known as the "Choral," the full perfection of his power and experience. Other musicians have composed symphonic works remarkable for varied excellences, but in Beethoven this form of writing seems to have attained its highest possibilities, and to have been illustrated by the greatest variety of effects, from the sublime to such as are simply beautiful and melodious. His hand swept the whole range of expression with unfaltering mastery. Some passages may seem obscure, some too elaborately wrought, some startling and abrupt, but on all is stamped the die of his great genius.

Beethoven's compositions for the piano, the sonatas, are no less notable for range and power of expression, their adaptation to meet all the varied moods of passion and sentiment. Other pianoforte composers have given us more warm and vivid color, richer sensual effects of tone, more wild and bizarre combination, perhaps even greater sweetness in melody; but we look in vain elsewhere for the spiritual passion and poetry, the aspiration and longing, the lofty humanity, which make the Beethoven sonatas the *suspiria de pro-fundis* of the composer's inner life. In addition to his symphonies and sonatas, he wrote the great opera of "Fidelio," and in the field of oratorio asserted his equality with Handel and Haydn by composing "The Mount of Olives." A great variety of chamber music, masses, and songs, bear the same imprint of power. He may be called the most original and conscientious of all the composers. Handel, Haydn, Mozart, Schubert, and Mendelssohn were inveterate thieves, and pilfered the choicest gems from old and forgotten writers without scruple. Beethoven seems to have been so fecund in great conceptions, so lifted on the wings of his tireless genius, so austere in artistic morality, that he stands for the most part above the reproach deservedly borne by his brother composers.

Beethoven's principal title to fame is in his superlative place as a symphonic composer. In the symphony music finds its highest intellectual dignity; in Beethoven the symphony has found its loftiest master.

SCHUBERT, SCHUMANN, AND FRANZ.
I.

Heinrich Heine, in his preface to a translation of "Don Quixote," discusses the creative powers of different peoples. To the Spaniard Cervantes is awarded the first place in novel-writing, and to our own Shakespeare, of course, the transcendent rank in drama.

"And the Germans," he goes on to say, "what palm is due to them? Well, we are the best writers of songs in the world. No people possesses such beautiful *Lieder* as the Germans. Just at present the nations have too much political business on hand; but, after that has once been settled, we Germans, English, Spaniards, Frenchmen, and Italians, will all go to the green forest and sing, and the nightingale shall be umpire. I feel sure that in this contest the song of Wolfgang Goethe will gain the prize."

There are few, if any, who will be disposed to dispute the verdict of the German poet, himself no mean rival, in depth and variety of lyric inspiration, even of the great Goethe. But a greater poet than either one of this great pair bears the suggestive and impersonal name of "The People." It is to the countless wealth of the German race in folk-songs, an affluence which can be traced back to the very dawn of civilization among them, that the possibility of such lyric poets as Goethe, Heine, Ruckert, and Uhland is due. From the days of the "Nibelungenlied," that great epic which, like the Homeric poems, can hardly be credited to any one author, every hamlet has rung with beautiful national songs, which sprung straight from the fervid heart of the people. These songs are balmy with the breath of the forest, the meadow, and river, and have that simple and bewitching freshness of motive and rhythm which unconsciously sets itself to music.

The German *Volkslied*, as the exponent of the popular heart, has a wide range, from mere comment on historical events, and quaint, droll satire, such as may be found in Hans Sachs, to the grand protest against spiritual bondage which makes the burden of Luther's hymn, "Ein' feste Burg." But nowhere is the beauty of the German song so marked as in those *Lieder* treating of love, deeds of arms, and the old mystic legends so dear to the German heart. Tieck writes of the "Minnesinger period:" "Believers sang of faith, lovers of love; knights described knightly actions and battles, and loving, believing knights were their chief audiences. The spring, beauty, gayety, were objects that could never tire; great duels and deeds of arms carried away every hearer, the more surely the stronger they were painted; and as the pillars and dome of the church encircled the flock, so did Religion, as the highest, encircle poetry and reality, and every heart in equal love humbled itself before her."

A similar spirit has always inspired the popular German song, a simple and beautiful reverence for the unknown, the worship of heroism, a vital sympathy with the various manifestations of Nature. Without the fire of the French *chansons*, the sonorous grace of the Tuscan *stornelli*, these artless ditties, with their exclusive reliance on true feeling, possess an indescribable charm.

The German *Lied* always preserved its characteristic beauty. Goethe, and the great school of lyric poets clustered around him, simply perfected the artistic form, without departing from the simplicity and soulfulness of the stock from which it came. Had it not been for the rich soil of popular song, we should not have had the peerless lyrics of modern Germany. Had it not been for the poetic inspiration of such word-makers as Goethe and Heine, we should not have had such music-makers in the sphere of song as Schubert and Franz.

The songs of these masters appeal to the interest and admiration of the world, then, not merely in virtue of musical beauty, but in that they are the most vital outgrowths of Teutonic nationality and feeling.

The immemorial melodies to which the popular songs of Germany were set display great simplicity of rhythm, even monotony, with frequent recurrence of the minor keys, so well adapted to express the melancholy tone of many of the poems. The strictly strophic treatment is used, or, in other words, the repetition of the melody of the first stanza in all the succeeding ones. The chasm between this and the varied form of the artistic modern song is deep and wide, yet it was overleaped in a single swift bound by the remarkable genius of Franz Schubert, who, though his compositions were many and matchless of their kind, died all too young; for, as the inscription on his tombstone pathetically has it, he was "rich in what he gave, richer in what he promised."

II.

The great masters of the last century tried their hands in the domain of song with only comparative success, partly because they did not fully realize the nature of this form of art, partly because they could not limit the sweep of the creative power within such narrow limits. Schubert was a revelation to his countrymen in his musical treatment of subjective passion, in his instinctive command over condensed, epigrammatic expression. This rich and gifted life, however quiet in its exterior facts, was great in its creative and spiritual manifestation. Born at Vienna of humble parents, January 31, 1797, the early life of Franz Schubert was commonplace in the extreme, the most interesting feature being the extraordinary development of his genius. At the age of fourteen he had made himself a master of counterpoint and harmony, and composed a large mass of chamber-music and works for the piano. His poverty was such that he was oftentimes unable to obtain the music-paper with which to fasten the immortal thoughts that thronged through his brain. It was two years later that his special creative function found exercise in the production of the two great songs, the "Erl-King" and the "Serenade," the former of which proved the source of most of the fame and money emolument he enjoyed during life. It is hardly needful to speak of the power and beauty of this composition, the weird sweetness of its melodies, the dramatic contrasts, the wealth of color and shading in its varying phrases, the subtilty of the accompaniment, which elaborates the spirit of the song itself. The piece was composed in less than an hour. One of Schubert's intimates tells us that he left him reading Goethe's great poem for the first time. He instantly conceived and arranged the melody, and when the friend returned after a short absence Schubert was rapidly noting the music from his head on paper. When the song was finished he rushed to the Stadtconvict school, his only *alma mater*, and sang it to the scholars. The music-master, Rucziszka, was overwhelmed with rapture and astonishment, and embraced the young composer in a transport of joy. When this immortal music was first sung to Goethe, the great poet said: "Had music, instead of words, been my instrument of thought, it is so I would have framed the legend."

The "Serenade" is another example of the swiftness of Schubert's artistic imagination. He and a lot of jolly boon-companions sat one Sunday afternoon in an obscure Viennese tavern, known as the Biersack. The surroundings were anything but conducive to poetic fancies—dirty tables, floor, and ceiling, the clatter of mugs and dishes, the loud dissonance of the beery German roisterers, the squalling of children, and all the sights and noises characteristic of the beer-cellar. One of our composer's companions had a volume of poems, which Schubert looked at in a lazy way, laughing and drinking the while. Singling out some verses, he said: "I have a pretty melody in my head for these lines, if I could only get a piece of ruled paper." Some staves were drawn on the back of a bill-of-fare, and here, amid all the confusion and riot, the divine melody of the "Serenade" was born, a tone-poem which embodies the most delicate dream of passion and tenderness that the heart of man ever conceived.

Both these compositions were eccentric and at odds with the old canons of song, fancied with a grace, warmth, and variety of color hitherto characteristic only of the more pretentious forms of music, which had already been brought to a great degree of perfection. They inaugurate the genesis of the new school of musical lyrics, the golden wedding of the union of poetry with music.

For a long time the young composer was unsuccessful in his attempts to break through the barren and irritating drudgery of a schoolmaster's life. At last a wealthy young dilettante, Franz von Schober, who had become an admirer of Schubert's songs, persuaded his mother to offer him a fixed home in her house. The latter gratefully accepted the overture of friendship, and thence became a daily guest at Schober's house. He made at this time a number of strong friendships with obscure poets, whose names only live through the music of the composer set to verses furnished by them; for Schubert, in his affluence of creative power, merely needed the slightest excuse for his genius to flow forth. But, while he wrote nothing that was not beautiful, his masterpieces are based only on themes furnished by the lyrics of such poets as Goethe, Heine, and Rilckert. It is related, in connection with his friendship with Mayrhofer, one of his rhyming associates of these days, that he would set the verses to music much faster than the other could compose them.

The songs of the obscure Schubert were gradually finding their way to favor among the exclusive circles of Viennese aristocracy. A celebrated singer of the opera, Vogl, though then far advanced in years, was much sought after for the drawing-room concerts so popular in Vienna, on account of the beauty of his art. Vogl was a warm admirer of Schubert's genius, and devoted himself assiduously to the task of interpreting it—a friendly office of no little value. Had it not been for this, our composer would have sunk to his early grave probably without even the small share of reputation and monetary return actually vouchsafed to him. The strange, dreamy unconsciousness of Schubert is very well illustrated in a story told by Vogl after his friend's death. One day Schubert left a new song at the singer's apartments, which, being too high, was transposed. Vogl, a fortnight afterward, sang it in the lower key to his friend, who remarked: "Really, that *Lied* is not so bad; who composed it?"

III.

Our great composer, from the peculiar constitution of his gifts, the passionate subjectiveness of his nature, might be supposed to have been peculiarly sensitive to the fascinations of love, for it is in this feeling that lyric inspiration has found its most fruitful root. But not so. Warmly susceptible to the charms of friendship, Schubert for the most part enacted the *rôle* of the woman-hater, which was not all affected; for the Hamletlike mood is only in part a simulated madness with souls of this type. In early youth he would sneer at the amours of his comrades. It is true he fell a victim to the charms of Theresa Grobe, a beautiful soprano, who afterward became the spouse of a master-baker. But the only genuine love-sickness of Schubert was of a far different type, and left indelible traces on his nature, as its very direction made it of necessity unfortunate. This was his attachment to Countess Caroline Esterhazy.

The Count Esterhazy, one of those great feudal princes still extant among the

Austrian nobility, took a traditional pride in encouraging genius, and found in Franz Schubert a noble object for the exercise of his generous patronage. He was almost a boy (only nineteen), except in the prodigious development of his genius, when he entered the Esterhazy family as teacher of music, though always treated as a dear and familiar friend. During the summer months, Schubert went with the Esterhazy s to their country-seat at Zelész, in Hungary. Here, amid beautiful scenery, and the sweetness of a social life perfect of its kind, our poet's life flew on rapid wings, the one bright, green spot of unalloyed happiness, for the dream was delicious while it lasted. Here, too, his musical life gathered a fresh inspiration, since he became acquainted with the treasures of the national Hungarian music, with its weird, wild rhythms and striking melodies. He borrowed the motives of many of his most characteristic songs from these reminiscences of hut and hall, for the Esterhazys were royal in their hospitality, and exercised a wide patriarchal sway.

The beautiful Countess Caroline, an enthusiastic girl of great beauty, became the object of a romantic passion. A young, inexperienced maiden, full of *naive* sweetness, the finest flower of the haughty Austrian caste, she stood at an infinite distance from Schubert, while she treated him with childlike confidence and fondness, laughing at his eccentricities, and worshiping his genius, lie bowed before this idol, and poured out all the incense of his heart. Schubert's exterior was anything but that of the ideal lover. Rude, unshapely features, thick nose, coarse, protruding mouth, and a shambling, awkward figure, were redeemed only by eyes of uncommon splendor and depth, aflame with the unmistakable light of the soul.

The inexperienced maiden hardly understood the devotion of the artist, which found expression in a thousand ways peculiar to himself. Only once he was on the verge of a full revelation. She asked him why he had dedicated nothing to her. With abrupt, passionate intensity of tone Schubert answered, "What's the use of that? Everything belongs to you!" This brink of confession seems to have frightened him, for it is said that after this he threw much more reserve about his intercourse with the family, till it was broken off. Hints in his letters, and the deep despondency which increased after this, indicate, however, that the humbly-born genius never forgot his beautiful dream.

He continued to pour out in careless profusion songs, symphonies, quartets, and operas, many of which knew no existence but in the score till after his death, hardly knowing of himself whether the productions had value or not. He created because it was the essential law of his being, and never paused to contemplate or admire the beauties of his own work. Schubert's body had been mouldering for several years, when his wonderful symphony in C major, one of the *chefs-d'oeuvre* of orchestral composition, was brought to the attention of the world by the critical admiration of Robert Schumann, who won the admiration of lovers of music, not less by his prompt vindication of neglected genius than by his own creative powers.

In the contest between Weber and Rossini which agitated Vienna, Schubert, though deeply imbued with the seriousness of art, and by nature closely allied in sympathies with the composer of "Der Freischütz," took no part. He was too easy-going to become a volunteer partisan, too shy and obscure to make his alliance a thing to be sought after. Besides, Weber had treated him with great brusqueness, and damned an opera for him, a slight which even good-natured Franz Schubert could not easily forgive.

The fifteen operas of Schubert, unknown now except to musicians, contain a wealth of beautiful melody which could easily be spread over a score of ordinary works. The purely lyric impulse so dominated him that dramatic arrangement was lost sight of, and the noblest melodies were likely to be lavished on the most unworthy situations. Even under the operatic form he remained essentially the song-writer. So in the symphony his affluence of melodic inspiration seems actually to embarrass him, to the detriment of that breadth and symmetry of treatment so vital to this form of art. It is in the musical lyric that our composer stands matchless.

During his life as an independent musician at Vienna, Schubert lived fighting a stern battle with want and despondency, while the publishers were commencing to make fortunes by the sale of his exquisite *Lieder*. At that time a large source of income for the Viennese composers was the public performance of their works in concerts under their own direction. From recourse to this, Schubert's bashfulness and lack of skill as a *virtuoso* on any instrument helped to bar him, though he accompanied his own songs with exquisite effect. Once only his friends organized a concert for him, and the success was very brilliant. But he was prevented from repeating the good fortune by that fatal illness which soon set in. So he lived out the last glimmers of his life, poverty-stricken, despondent, with few even of the amenities of friendship to soothe his declining days. Yet those who know the beautiful results of that life, and have even a faint glow of sympathy with the life of a man of genius, will exclaim with one of the most eloquent critics of Schubert:

"But shall we, therefore, pity a man who all the while reveled in the treasures of his creative ore, and from the very depths of whose despair sprang the sweetest flowers of song? Who would not battle with the iciest blast of the north if out of storm and snow he could bring back to his chamber the germs of the 'Winterreise?' Who would grudge the moisture of his eyes if he could render it immortal in the strains of Schubert's 'Lob der Thrâne?'"

Schubert died in the flower of his youth, November 19, 1828; but he left behind him nearly a thousand compositions, six hundred of which were songs. Of his operas only the "Enchanted Harp" and "Rosamond" were put on the stage during his lifetime. "Fierabras," considered to be his finest dramatic work, has never been produced. His church music, consisting of six masses, many offertories, and the great "Hallelujah" of Klopstock, is still performed in Germany. Several of his symphonies are ranked among the greatest works of this nature. His pianoforte compositions are brilliant, and strongly in the style of Beethoven, who was always the great object of Schubert's devoted admiration, his artistic idol and model. It was his dying request that he should be buried by the side of Beethoven, of whom the art-world had been deprived the year before.

Compared with Schubert, other composers seem to have written in prose. His imagination burned with a passionate love of Nature. The lakes, the woods, the mountain heights, inspired him with eloquent reveries that burst into song; but he always saw Nature through the medium of human passion and sympathy, which transfigured it. He was the faithful interpreter of spiritual suffering, and the joy which is born thereof.

The genius of Schubert seems to have been directly formed for the expression of subjective emotion in music. That his life should have been simultaneous with the perfect literary unfolding of the old *Volkslied* in the superb lyrics of Goethe, Heine, and their school, is quite remarkable. Poe-try and song clasped hands on the same lofty summits of genius. Liszt has given to our composer the title of *le musicien le plus poétique*, which very well expresses his place in art.

In the song as created by Schubert and transmitted to his successors, there are three forms, the first of which is that of the simple *Lied*, with one unchanged melody. A good example of this is the setting of Goethe's "Haideroslein," which is full of quaint grace and simplicity. A second and more elaborate method is what the Germans call "through-composed," in which all the different feelings are successively embodied in the changes of the melody, the sense of unity being preserved by the treatment of the accompaniment, or the recurrence of the principal motive at the close of the song. Two admirable models of this are found in the "Lindenbaum" and "Serenade."

The third and finest art-method, as applied by Schubert to lyric music, is the "declamatory." In this form we detect the consummate flower of the musical lyric. The vocal part is lifted into a species of passionate chant, full of dramatic fire and color, while the accompaniment, which is extremely elaborate, furnishes a most picturesque setting. The genius of the composer displays itself here fully as much as in the vocal treatment. When the lyric feeling rises to its climax it expresses itself in the crowning melody, this high tide of the music and poetry being always in unison. As masterpieces of this form may be cited "Die Stadt" and "Der Erlkönig," which stand far beyond any other works of the same nature in the literature of music.

IV.

Robert Schumann, the loving critic, admirer, and disciple of Schubert in the province of song, was in most respects a man of far different type. The son of a man of wealth and position, his mind and tastes were cultivated from early youth with the utmost care. Schumann is known in Germany no less as a philosophical thinker and critic than as a composer. As the editor of the *Neue Zeitschrift für Musik*, he exercised a powerful influence over contemporary thought in art-matters, and established himself both as a keen and incisive thinker and as a master of literary style. Schumann was at first intended for the law, but his unconquerable taste for music asserted itself in spite of family opposition. His acquaintance with the celebrated teacher Wieck, whose gifted daughter Clara afterward became his wife, finally established his career; for it was through Wieck's advice that the Schumann family yielded their opposition to the young man's bent.

Once settled in his new career, Schumann gave himself up to work with the most indefatigable ardor. The early part of the present century was a halcyon time for the *virtuosi*, and the fame and wealth that poured themselves on such players as Paganini and Liszt made such a pursuit tempting in the extreme. Fortunately, the young musician was saved from such a career. In his zeal of practice and desire to attain a perfectly independent action for each finger on the piano, Schumann devised some machinery, the result of which was to weaken the sinews of his third finger by undue distention. By this he lost the effective use of the whole right hand, and of course his career as a *virtuoso* practically closed.

Music gained in its higher walks what it lost in a lower. Schumann devoted himself to composition and aesthetic criticism, after he had passed through a thorough course of preparatory studies. Both as a writer and a composer Schumann fought against Philistinism in music. Ardent, progressive, and imaginative, he soon became the leader of the romantic school, and inaugurated the crusade which had its parallel in France in that carried on by Victor Hugo in the domain of poetry. His early pianoforte compositions bear the strong impress of this fiery, revolutionary spirit. His great symphonic works belong to a later period, when his whole nature had mellowed and ripened without losing its imaginative sweep and brilliancy. Schumann's compositions for the piano and orchestra are those by which his name is most widely honored, but nowhere do we find a more characteristic exercise of his genius than in his songs, to which this article will call more special attention.

Such works as the "Etudes Symphoniques" and the "Kreisleriana" express much of the spirit of unrest and longing aspiration, the struggle to get away from prison-bars and limits, which seem to have sounded the key-note of Schumann's deepest nature. But these feelings could only find their fullest outlet in the musical form expressly suited to subjective emotion. Accordingly, the "Sturm and Drang" epoch of his life, when all his thoughts and conceptions were most unsettled and visionary, was most fruitful in lyric song. In Heinrich Heine he found a fitting poetical co-worker, in whose moods he seemed to see a perfect reflection of his own—Heine, in whom the bitterest irony was wedded to the deepest pathos, "the spoiled favorite of the Graces," "the knight with the laughing tear in his scutcheon"—Heine, whose songs are charged with the brightest light and deepest gloom of the human heart.

Schumann's songs never impress us as being deliberate attempts at creative effort, consciously selected forms through which to express thoughts struggling for speech. They are rather involuntary experiments to relieve one's self of some wo-ful burden, medicine for the soul. Schumann is never distinctively the lyric composer; his imagination had too broad and majestic a wing. But in those moods, peculiar to genius, where the soul is flung back on itself with a sense of impotence, our composer instinctively burst into song. He did not in the least advance or change its artistic form, as fixed by Schubert. This, indeed, would have been irreconcilable with his use of the song as a simple medium of personal feeling, an outlet and safeguard.

The peculiar place of Schumann as a songwriter is indicated by his being called the musical exponent of Heine, who seems to be the other half of his soul. The composer enters into each shade and detail of the poet's meaning with an intensity and fidelity which one can never cease admiring. It is this phase which gives the Schumann songs their great artistic value. In their clean-cut, abrupt, epigrammatic force there is something different from the work of any other musical lyrist. So much has this impressed the students of the composer that more than one able critic has ventured to prophesy that Schumann's greatest claim to immortality would yet be found in such works as the settings of "Ich grolle nicht" and the "Dichterliebe" series—a perverted estimate, perhaps, but with a large substratum of truth. The duration of Schumann's song-time was short, the greater part of his *Lieder* having been written in 1840. After this he gave himself up to oratorio, symphony, and chamber-music.

V.

Among the contemporary masters of the musical lyric, the most shining name is that of Robert Franz, a marked individuality, and, though indirectly moulded by the influence of Schubert and Schumann, a creative mind of a striking type.

The art-impulse, strikingly characteristic of Franz as a song composer, or, perhaps, to express it more accurately, the art-limitation, is that the musical inspiration is directly dependent on the poetic strength of the *Lied*. He would be utterly at a loss to treat a poem which lacked beauty and force. With but little command over absolute music, that flow of melody which pours from some natures like a perennial spring, the poetry of word is necessary to evoke poetry of tone.

Robert Franz, like Schumann, was embarrassed in his youth by the bitter opposition of his family to his adoption of music, and, like the great apostle of romantic music, his steady perseverance wore it out. He made himself a severe student of the great masters, and rapidly acquired a deep knowledge of the mysteries of harmony and counterpoint. There are no songs with such intricate and difficult accompaniments, though always vital to the lyrical motive, as those of Robert Franz. For a long time, even after he felt himself fully equipped, Franz refrained from artistic production, waiting till the processes of fermenting and clarifying should end, in the mean while promising he would yet have a word to say for himself.

With him, as with many other men of genius, the blow which broke the seal of inspiration was an affair of the heart. He loved a beautiful and accomplished woman, but loved unfortunately. The catastrophe ripened him into artistic maturity, and the very first effort of his lyric power was marked by surprising symmetry and fullness of power. He wrote to give overflow to his deep feelings, and the song came from his heart of hearts. Robert Schumann, the generous critic, gave this first work an enthusiastic welcome, and the young composer leaped into reputation at a bound. Of the four hundred or more songs written by Robert Franz, there are perhaps fifty which rank as masterpieces. His life has passed devoid of incident, though rich in spiritual insight and passion, as his *Lieder* unmistakably show. Though the instrumental setting of this composer's songs is so elaborate and beautiful oftentimes, we frequently find him at his best in treating words full of the simplicity and *naïveté* of the old *Volkslied*. Many of his songs are set to the poems of Robert Burns, one of the few British poets who have been able to give their works the subtile singing quality which comes not merely of the rhythm but of the feeling of the verse. Heine also furnished him with the themes of many of his finest songs, for this poet has been an inexhaustible treasure-trove to the modern lyric composer. One of the most striking features of Franz as a composer is found in the delicate light and shade, introduced into the songs by the simplest means, which none but the man of genius would think of; for it is the great artist who attains his ends through the simplest effects.

While the same atmosphere of thought and feeling is felt in the spiritual life of Robert Franz which colored the artistic being of Schubert and Schumann, there is a certain repose and balance all his own. We get the idea of one never carried away by his genius, or delivering passionate utterances from the Delphic tripod, but the master of all his powers, the conscious and skillful ruler of his own inspirations. If the sense of spontaneous freshness is sometimes lost, perhaps there is a gain in breadth and finish. If Schubert has unequaled melody and dramatic force, Schumann drastic and pointed intensity, Robert Franz deserves the palm for the finish and symmetry of his work.

Of the great song composers, Franz Schubert is the unquestioned master. To him the modern artistic song owes its birth, and, as in the myth of Pallas, we find birth and maturity simultaneous. It bloomed at once into perfect flower, and the wrorld will probably never see any essential advances in it. It is this form of music which appeals most widely to the human heart, to old and young, high and low, learned and ignorant. It has "the one touch of Nature which makes the whole world kin." Even the mind not attuned to sympathy with the more elaborate forms of music is soothed and delighted by it; for—

"It is old and plain;
The spinsters and the knitters in the sun,
And the free maids that weave their thread with bones,
Do use to chant it; it is silly sooth,
And dallies with the innocence of love
Like the old age."

CHOPIN.

I.

Never has Paris, the Mecca of European art, genius, and culture, presented a more brilliant social spectacle than it did in 1832. Hither ward came pilgrims from all countries, poets, painters, and musicians, anxious to breathe the inspiring air of the French capital, where society laid its warmest homage at the feet of the artist. Here came, too, in dazzling crowds, the rich nobles and the beautiful women of Europe to find the pleasure, the freedom, the joyous unrestraint, with which Paris offers its banquet of sensuous and intellectual delights to the hungry epicure. Then as now the queen of the art-world, Paris absorbed and assimilated to herself the most brilliant influences in civilization.

In all of brilliant Paris there was no more charming and gifted circle than that which gathered around the young Polish pianist and composer, Chopin, then a recent arrival in the gay city. His peculiarly original genius, his weird and poetic style of playing, which transported his hearers into a mystic fairy-land of sunlight and shadow, his strangely delicate beauty, the alternating reticence and enthusiasm of his manners, made him the idol of the clever men and women, who courted the society of the shy and sensitive musician; for to them he was a fresh revelation. Dr. Franz Liszt gives the world some charming pictures of this art-coterie, which was wont often to assemble at Chopin's rooms in the Chaussée d'Antin.

His room, taken by surprise, is all in darkness except the luminous ring thrown off by the candles on the piano, and the flashes flickering from the fireplace. The guests gather around informally as the piano sighs, moans, murmurs, or dreams under the fingers of the player. Hein-rich Heine, the most poetic of humorists, leans on the instrument, and asks, as he listens to the music and watches the firelight, "if the roses always glowed with a flame so triumphant? if the trees at moonlight sang always so harmoniously?" Meyerbeer, one of the musical giants, sits near at hand lost in reverie; for he forgets his own great harmonies, forged with hammer of Cyclops, listening to the dreamy passion and poetry woven into such quaint fabrics of sound.

Adolphe Nourrit, passionate and ascetic, with the spirit of some mediaeval monastic painter, an enthusiastic servant of art in its purest, severest form, a combination of poet and anchorite, is also there; for he loves the gentle musician, who seems to be a visitor from the world of spirits. Eugène Delacroix, one of the greatest of modern painters, his keen eyes half closed in meditation, absorbs the vague mystery of color which imagination translates from the harmony, and attains new insight and inspiration through the bright links of suggestion by which one art lends itself to another. The two great Polish poets, Nierncewicz and Mickiewicz (the latter the Dante of the Slavic race), exiles from their unhappy land, feed their sombre sorrow, and find in the wild, Oriental rhythms of the player only melancholy memories of the past. Perhaps Victor Hugo, Balzac, Lamartine, or the aged Chateaubriand, also drop in by-and-by, to recognize, in the music, echoes of the daring romanticism which they opposed to the classic and formal pedantry of the time.

Buried in a fauteuil, with her arms resting upon a table, sits Mme. George Sand (that name so tragically mixed with Chopin's life), "curiously attentive, gracefully subdued." With the second sight of genius, which pierces through the mask, she saw the sweetness, the passion, the delicate emotional sensibility of Chopin; and her insatiate nature must unravel and assimilate this new study in human enjoyment and suffering. She had then just finished "Lelia," that strange and powerful creation, in which she embodied all her hatred of the forms and tyrannies of society, her craving for an impossible social ideal, her tempestuous hopes and desires, in such startling types. Exhausted by the struggle, she panted for the rest and luxury of a companionship in which both brain and heart could find sympathy. She met Chopin, and she recognized in the poetry of his temperament and the fire of his genius what she desired. Her personality, electric, energetic, and imperious, exercised the power of a magnet on the frail organization of Chopin, and he loved once and forever, with a passion that consumed him; for in Mme. Sand he found the blessing and curse of his life. This many-sided woman, at this point of her development, found in the fragile Chopin one phase of her nature which had never been expressed, and he was sacrificed to the demands of an insatiable originality, which tried all things in turn, to be contented with nothing but an ideal which could never be attained.

About the time of Chopin's arrival in Paris the political effervescence of the recent revolution had passed into art and letters. It was the oft-repeated battle of Romanticism against Classicism. There could be no truce between those who believed that everything must be fashioned after old models, that Procrustes must settle the height and depth, the length and breadth of art-forms, and those who, inspired with the new wine of liberty and free creative thought, held that the rule of form should always be the mere expression of the vital, flexible thought. The one side argued that supreme perfection already reached left the artist hope only in imitation; the other, that the immaterial beautiful could have no fixed absolute form. Victor Hugo among the poets, Delacroix among the painters, and Berlioz among the musicians, led the ranks of the romantic school.

Chopin found himself strongly enlisted in this contest on the side of the new school. His free, unconventional nature found in its teachings a musical atmosphere true to the artistic and political proclivities of his native Poland; for Chopin breathed the spirit and tendencies of his people in every fibre of his soul, both as man and artist. Our musician, however, in freeing himself from all servile formulas, sternly repudiated the charlatanism which would replace old abuses with new ones.

Chopin, in his views of his art, did not admit the least compromise with those who failed earnestly to represent progress, nor, on the other hand, with those who sought to make their art a mere profitable trade. With him, as with all the great musicians, his art was a religion—something so sacred that it must be approached with unsullied heart and hand. This reverential feeling was shown in the following touching fact: It was a Polish custom to choose the garments in which one would be buried. Chopin, though among the first of contemporary artists, gave fewer concerts than any other; but, notwithstanding this, he left directions to be borne to the grave in the clothes he had worn on such occasions.

II.

Frederick Francis Chopin was born near Warsaw, in 1810, of French extraction. He learned music at the age of nine from Ziwny, a pupil of Sebastian Bach, but does not seem to have impressed any one with his remarkable talent except Madame Catalani, the great singer, who gave him a watch. Through the kindness of Prince Radziwill, an enthusiastic patron of art, he was sent to Warsaw College, where his genius began to unfold itself. He afterward became a pupil of the Warsaw Conservatory, and acquired there a splendid mastery over the science of music. His labor was prodigious in spite of his frail health; and his knowledge of contrapuntal forms was such as to exact the highest encomiums from his instructors.

Through his brother pupils he was introduced to the highest Polish society, for his fellows bore some of the proudest names in Poland. Chopin seems to have absorbed the peculiarly romantic spirit of his race, the wild, imaginative melancholy, which, almost gloomy in the Polish peasant, when united to grace and culture in the Polish noble, offered an indescribable social charm. Balzac sketches the Polish woman in these picturesque antitheses: "Angel through love, demon through fantasy; child through faith, sage through experience; man through the brain, woman through the heart; giant through hope, mother through sorrow; and poet through dreams." The Polish gentleman was chivalrous, daring, and passionate; the heir of the most gifted and brilliant of the Slavic races, with a proud heritage of memory which gave his bearing an indescribable dignity, though the son of a fallen nation. Ardently devoted to pleasure, the Poles embodied in their national dances wild and inspiring rhythms, a glowing poetry of sentiment as well as motion, which mingled with their Bacchanal fire a chaste and lofty meaning that became at times funereal. Polish society at this epoch pulsated with an originality, an imagination, and a romance, which transfigured even the common things of life.

It was amid such an atmosphere that Chopin's early musical career was spent, and his genius received its lasting impress. One afternoon in after-years he was playing to one of the most distinguished women in Paris, and she said that his music suggested to her those gardens in Turkey where bright parterres of flowers and shady bowers were strewed with gravestones and burial mounds.

This underlying depth of melancholy Chopin's music expresses most eloquently, and it may be called the perfect artistic outcome of his people; for in his sweetest tissues of sound the imagination can detect agitation, rancor, revolt, and menace, sometimes despair. Chateaubriand dreamed of an Eve innocent, yet fallen; ignorant of all, yet knowing all; mistress, yet virgin. He found this in a Polish girl of seventeen, whom he paints as a "mixture of Odalisque and Valkyr." The romantic and fanciful passion of the Poles, bold, yet unworldly, is shown in the habit of drinking the health of a sweetheart from her own shoe.

Chopin, intensely spiritual by temperament and fragile in health, born an enthusiast, was colored through and through with the rich dyes of Oriental passion; but with these were mingled the fantastic and ideal elements which,

"Wrapped in sense, yet dreamed of heavenlier joys."

And so he went to Paris, the city of his fate, ripe for the tragedy of his life. After the revolution of 1830, he started to go to London, and, as he said, "passed through Paris." Yet Paris he did not leave till he left it with Mme. Sand to live a brief dream of joy in the beautiful isle of Majorca.

III.

Liszt describes Chopin in these words: "His blue eyes were more spiritual than dreamy; his bland smile never writhed into bitterness. The transparent delicacy of his complexion pleased the eye; his fair hair was soft and silky; his nose slightly aquiline; his bearing so distinguished, and his manners stamped with such high breeding, that involuntarily he was always treated *en prince*. His gestures were many and graceful; the tones of his voice veiled, often stifled. His stature was low, his limbs were slight." Again, Mme. Sand paints him even more characteristically in her novel "Lucrezia Floriani:" "Gentle, sensitive, and very lovely, he united the charm of adolescence with the suavity of a more mature age; through the want of muscular development he retained a peculiar beauty, an exceptional physiognomy, which, if we may venture so to speak, belonged to neither age nor sex.... It was more like the ideal creations with which the poetry of the middle ages adorned the Christian temples. The delicacy of his constitution rendered him interesting in the eyes of women. The full yet graceful cultivation of his mind, the sweet and captivating originality of his conversation, gained for him the attention of the most enlightened men; while those less highly cultivated liked him for the exquisite courtesy of his manners."

All this reminds us of Shelley's dream of Hermaphroditus, or perhaps of Shelley himself, for Chopin was the Shelley of music.

His life in Paris was quiet and retired. The most brilliant and beautiful women desired to be his pupils, but Chopin refused except where he recognized in the petitioners exceptional earnestness and musical talent. He gave but few concerts, for his genius could not cope with great masses of people. He said to Liszt: "I am not suited for concert-giving. The public intimidate me, their breath stifles me. You are destined for it; for when you do not gain your public, you have the force to assault, to overwhelm, to compel them." It was his delight to play to a few chosen friends, and to evoke for them such dreams from the ivory gate, which Virgil fabled to be the portal of Elysium, as to make his music

"The silver key of the fountain of tears,
Where the spirit drinks till the brain is wild:
Softest grave of a thousand fears,
Where their mother, Care, like a weary child,
Is laid asleep in a bed of flowers."

He avoided general society, finding in the great artists and those sympathetic with art his congenial companions. His life was given up to producing those unique compositions which make him, *par excellence*, the king of the pianoforte. He was recognized by Liszt, Kalkbrenner, Pie y el, Field, and Meyerbeer, as being the most wonderful of players; yet he seemed to disdain such a reputation as a cheap notoriety, ceasing to appear in public after the first few concerts, which produced much excitement and would have intoxicated most performers. He sought largely the society of the Polish exiles, men and women of the highest rank who had thronged to Paris.

His sister Louise, whom he dearly loved, frequently came to Paris from Warsaw to see him; and he kept up a regular correspondence with his own family. Yet he abhorred writing so much that he would go to any shifts to avoid answering a note. Some of his beautiful countrywomen, however, possess precious memorials in the shape of letters written in Polish, which he loved much more than French. His thoughtfulness was continually sending pleasant little gifts and souvenirs to his Warsaw friends. This tenderness and consideration displayed itself too in his love of children. He would spend whole evenings in playing blind-man's-buff or telling them charming fairy-stories from the folk-lore in which Poland is singularly rich.

Always gentle, he yet knew how to rebuke arrogance, and had sharp repartees for those who tried to force him into musical display. On one occasion, when he had just left the dining-room, an indiscreet host, who had had the simplicity to promise his guests some piece executed by him as a rare dessert, pointed him to an open piano. Chopin quietly refused, but on being pressed said, with a languid and sneering drawl: "Ah, sir, I have just dined; your hospitality, I see, demands payment."

IV.

Mme. Sand, in her "Lettres d'un Voyageur," depicts the painful lethargy which seizes the artist when, having incorporated the emotion which inspired him in his work, his imagination still remains under the dominance of the insatiate idea, without being able to find a new incarnation. She was suffering in this way when the character of Chopin excited her curiosity and suggested a healthful and happy relief. Chopin dreaded to meet this modern Sibyl. The superstitious awe he felt was a premonition whose meaning was hidden from him. They met, and Chopin lost his fear in one of those passions which feed on the whole being with a ceaseless hunger.

In the fall of 1837 Chopin yielded to a severe attack of the disease which was hereditary in his frame. In company with Mme. Sand, who had become his constant companion, he went to the isle of Majorca, to find rest and medicine in the balmy breezes of the Mediterranean. All the happiness of Chopin's life was gathered in the focus of this experience. He had a most loving and devoted nurse, who yielded to all his whims, soothed his fretfulness, and watched over him as a mother does over a child. The grounds of the villa where they lived were as perfect as Nature and art could make them, and exquisite scenes greeted the eye at every turn. Here they spent long golden days.

The feelings of Chopin for his gifted companion are best painted by herself in the pages of "Lucrezia Floriani," where she is the "Floriani," Liszt "Count Salvator Albani," and Chopin "Prince Karol:" "It seemed as if this fragile being was absorbed and consumed by the strength of his affection.... But he loved for the sake of loving.... His love was his life, and, delicious or bitter, he had not the power of withdrawing himself a single moment from its domination." Slowly she nursed him back into temporary health, and in the sunlight of her love his mind assumed a gayety and cheerfulness it had never known before.

It had been the passionate hope of Chopin to marry Mme. Sand, but wedlock was alien alike to her philosophy and preference. After a protracted intimacy, she wearied of his persistent entreaties, or perhaps her self-development had exhausted what it sought in the poet-musician. An absolute separation came, and his mistress buried the episode in her life with the epitaph: "Two natures, one rich in its exuberance, the other in its exclusiveness, could never really mingle, and a whole world separated them." Chopin said: "All the cords that bind me to life are broken." His sad summary of all was that his life had been an episode which began and ended in Paris. What a contrast to the being of a few years before, of whom it is written: "He was no longer on the earth; he was in an empyrean of golden clouds and perfumes; his imagination, so full of exquisite beauty, seemed engaged in a monologue with God himself!"*

* "Lucrezia Floriani."

Both Liszt and Mme. Dudevant have painted Chopin somewhat as a sickly sentimentalist, living in an atmosphere of moonshine and unreality. Yet this was not precisely true. In spite of his delicacy of frame and romantic imagination, Chopin was never ill till within the last ten years of his life, when the seeds of hereditary consumption developed themselves. As a young man he was lively and joyous, always ready for frolic, and with a great fund of humor, especially in caricature. Students of human character know how consistent these traits are with a deep undercurrent of melancholy, which colors the whole life when the immediate impulse of joy subsides.

From the date of 1840 Chopin's health declined; but through the seven years during which his connection with Mme. Sand continued, he persevered actively in his work of composition. The final rupture with the woman he so madly loved seems to have been his death-blow. He spoke of Mme. Sand without bitterness, but his soul pined in the bitter-sweet of memory. He recovered partially, and spent a short season of concert-giving in London, where he was feted and caressed by the best society as he had been in Paris. Again he was sharply assailed by his fatal malady, and he returned to Paris to die. Let us describe one of his last earthly experiences, on Sunday, the 15th of October, 1849.

Chopin had lain insensible from one of his swooning attacks for some time. His sister Louise was by his side, and the Countess Delphine Potocka, his beautiful countrywoman and a most devoted friend, watched him with streaming eyes. The dying musician became conscious, and faintly ordered a piano to be rolled in from the adjoining room. He turned to the countess, and whispered, feebly, "Sing." She had a lovely voice, and, gathering herself for the effort, she sang that famous canticle to the Virgin which, tradition says, saved Stradella's life from assassins. "How beautiful it is!" he exclaimed. "My God! how very beautiful!" Again she sang to him, and the dying musician passed into a trance, from which he never fully aroused till he expired, two days afterward, in the arms of his pupil, M. Gutman.

Chopin's obsequies took place at the Madeleine Church, and Lablache sang on this occasion the same passage, the "Tuba Mirum" of Mozart's Requiem Mass, which he had sung at the funeral of Beethoven in 1827; while the other solos were given by Mme. Viardot Garcia and Mme. Castellan. He lies in Père Lachaise, beside Cherubini and Bellini.

V.

The compositions of Chopin were exclusively for the piano; and alike as composer and virtuoso he is the founder of a new school, or perhaps may be said to share that honor with Robert Schumann—the school which to-day is represented in its advanced form by Liszt and Von Billow. Schumann called him "the boldest and proudest poetic spirit of the times." In addition to this remarkable poetic power, he was a splendidly-trained musician, a great adept in style, and one of the most original masters of rhythm and harmony that the records of music show. All his works, though wanting in breadth and robustness of tone, are characterized by the utmost finish and refinement. Full of delicate and unexpected beauties, elaborated with the finest touch, his effects are so quaint and fresh as to fill the mind of the listener with pleasurable sensations, perhaps not to be derived from grander works.

Chopin was essentially the musical exponent of his nation; for he breathed in all the forms of his art the sensibilities, the fires, the aspirations, and the melancholy of the Polish race. This is not only evident in his polonaises, his waltzes and mazurkas, in which the wild Oriental rhythms of the original dances are treated with the creative skill of genius; but also in the *études*, the preludes, nocturnes, scherzos, ballads, etc., with which he so enriched musical literature. His genius could never confine itself within classic bonds, but, fantastic and impulsive, swayed and bent itself with easy grace to inspirations that were always novel and startling, though his boldness was chastened by deep study and fine art-sense.

All of the suggestions of the quaint and beautiful Polish dance-music were worked by Chopin into a variety of forms, and were greatly enriched by his skill in handling. He dreamed out his early reminiscences in music, and these national memories became embalmed in the history of art. The polonaises are marked by the fire and ardor of his soldier race, and the mazurkas are full of the coquetry and tenderness of his countrywomen; while the ballads are a free and powerful rendering of Polish folk-music, beloved alike in the herdsman's hut and the palace of the noble. In deriving his inspiration direct from the national heart, Chopin did what Schumann, Schubert, and Weber did in Germany, what Rossini did in Italy, and shares with them a freshness of melodic power to be derived from no other source. Rather tender and elegiac than vigorous, the deep sadness underlying the most sparkling forms of his work is most notable. One can at times almost recognize the requiem of a nation in the passionate melancholy on whose dark background his fancy weaves such beautiful figures and colors.

Franz Liszt, in characterizing Chopin as a composer, furnishes an admirable study: "We meet with beauties of a high order, expressions entirely new, and a harmonic tissue as original as erudite. In his compositions boldness is always justified; richness, often exuberance, never interferes with clearness; singularity never degenerates into the uncouth and fantastic; the sculpturing is never disordered; the luxury of ornament never overloads the chaste eloquence of the principal lines. His best works abound in combinations which may be said to be an epoch in the handling of musical style. Daring, brilliant, and attractive, they disguise their profundity under so much grace, their science under so many charms, that it is with difficulty we free ourselves sufficiently from their magical inthrallment, to judge coldly of their theoretical value."

As a romance composer Chopin struck out his own path, and has no rival. Full of originality, his works display the utmost dignity and refinement. He revolted from the bizarre and eccentric, though the peculiar influences which governed his development might well have betrayed one less finely organized.

As a musical poet, embodying the feelings and tendencies of a people, Chopin advances his chief claim to his place in art. He did not task himself to be a national musician; for he is utterly without pretense and affectation, and sings spontaneously without design or choice, from the fullness of a rich nature. He collected "in luminous sheaves the impressions felt everywhere through his country—vaguely felt, it is true, yet in fragments pervading all hearts."

Chopin was repelled by the lusty and almost coarse humor sometimes displayed by Schubert, for he was painfully fastidious. He could not fully understand nor appreciate Beethoven, whose works are full of lion-marrow, robust and masculine alike in conception and treatment. He did not admire Shakespeare, because his great delineations are too vivid and realistic. Our musician was essentially a dreamer and idealist. His range was limited, but within it he reached perfection of finish and originality never surpassed. But, with all his limitations, the art-judgment of the world places him high among those

".... whom Art's service pure
Hallows and claims, whose hearts are made her throne,
"Whose lips her oracle, ordained secure
To lead a priestly life and feed the ray
Of her eternal shrine; to them alone
Her glorious countenance unveiled is shown."

WEBER.

I.

The genius which inspired the three great works, "Der Freischutz," "Euryanthe," and "Oberon," has stamped itself as one of the most original and characteristic in German music. Full of bold and surprising strokes of imagination, these operas are marked by the true atmosphere of national life and feeling, and Ave feel in them the fresh, rich color of the popular traditions, and song-music which make the German *Lieder* such an inexhaustible treasure-trove. As Weber was maturing into that fullness of power which gave to the world his greater works, Germany had been wrought into a passionate patriotism by the Napoleonic wars. The call to arms resounded from one end of the Fatherland to the other. Every hamlet thrilled with fervor, and all the resources of national tradition were evoked to heighten the love of country into a puissance which should save the land. Germany had been humiliated by a series of crushing defeats, and national pride was stung to vindicate the grand old memories. France, in answer to a similar demand for some art-expression of its patriotism, had produced its Rouget de-Lisle; Germany produced the poet Korner and the musician Weber.

It is not easy to appreciate the true quality and significance of Weber's art-life without considering the peculiar state of Germany at the time; for if ever creative imagination was forged and fashioned by its environments into a logical expression of public needs and impulses, it was in the case of the father of German romantic opera. This inspiration permeated the whole soil of national thought, and its embodiment in art and letters has hardly any parallel except in that brilliant morning of English thought which we know as the Elizabethan era. To understand Weber the composer, then, we must think of him not only as the musician, but as the patriot and revivalist of ancient tendencies in art, drawn directly from the warm heart of the people.

Karl Maria von Weber was born at Eutin, in Holstein, December 18, 1786. His father had been a soldier, but, owing to extravagance and folly, had left the career of arms, and, being an educated musician, had become by turns attached to an orchestra, director of a theatre, Kapellmeister, and wandering player—never remaining long in one position, for he was essentially vagrant and desultory in character. Whatever Karl Maria had to suffer from his father's folly and eccentricity, he was indebted to him for an excellent training in the art of which he was to become so brilliant an ornament. He had excellent masters in singing and the piano, as also in drawing and engraving. So he grew up a melancholy, imaginative, recluse, absorbed in his studies, and living in a dream-land of his own, which he peopled with ideal creations. His passionate love of Nature, tinged with old German superstition, planted in his imagination those fruitful germs which bore such rich results in after-years.

In 1797 Weber studied the piano and composition under Ilanschkel, a thoroughly scientific musician, and found in his severe drill a happy counter-balancing influence to the more desultory studies which had preceded. Major Weber's restless tendencies did not permit his family to remain long in one place. In 1798 they moved to Salzburg, where young Weber was placed at the musical institute of which Michael Haydn, brother of the great Joseph, was director. Here a variety of misfortunes assailed the Weber family. Major Franz Anton was unsuccessful in all his theatrical undertakings, and extreme poverty stared them all in the face. The gentle mother, too, whom Karl so dearly loved, sickened and died. This was a terrible blow to the affectionate boy, from which he did not soon recover.

The next resting-place in the pilgrimage of the Weber family was Munich, where Major Weber, who, however flagrant his shortcomings in other ways, was resolved that the musical powers of his son should be thoroughly trained, placed him under the care of the organist Kalcher for studies in composition.

For several years, Karl was obliged to lead the same shifting, nomadic sort of life, never stopping long, but dragged hither and thither in obedience to his father's vagaries and necessities, but always studying under the best masters who could be obtained. While under Kalcher, several masses, sonatas, trios, and an opera, "Die Macht der Liebe und des Weins" ("The Might of Love and Wine"), were written. Another opera, "Das Waldmäd-chen" ("The Forest Maiden"), was composed and produced when he was fourteen; and two years later in Salzburg he composed "Peter Schmoll und seine Nachbarn," an operetta, which exacted warm praise from Michael Haydn.

At the age of seventeen he became the pupil of the great teacher Abbé Vogler, under whose charge also Meyerbeer was then studying. Our young composer worked with great assiduity under the able instruction of Vogier, who was of vast service in bringing the chaos of his previous contradictory teachings into order and light. All these musical *Wanderjahre*, however trying, had steeled Karl Maria into a stern self-reliance, and he found in his skill as an engraver the means to remedy his father's wastefulness and folly.

II.

A curious episode in Weber's life was his connection with the royal family of Wurtemberg, where he found a dissolute, poverty-stricken court, and a whimsical, arrogant, half-crazy king. Here he remained four years in a half-official musical position, his nominal duty being that of secretary to the king's brother, Prince Ludwig. This part of his career was almost a sheer waste, full of dreary and irritating experiences, which Weber afterward spoke of with disgust and regret. His spirit revolted from the capricious tyranny which he was obliged to undergo, but circumstances seem to have coerced him into a protracted endurance of the place. His letters tell us how bitterly he detested the king and his dull, pompous court, though Prince Ludwig in a way seemed to have been attached to his secretary. One of his biographers says:

"Weber hated the king, of whose wild caprice and vices he witnessed daily scenes, before whose palace-gates he was obliged to slink bareheaded, and who treated him with unmerited ignominy. Sceptre and crown had never been imposing objects in his eyes, unless worn by a worthy man; and consequently he was wont, in the thoughtless levity of youth, to forget the dangers he ran, and to answer the king with a freedom of tone which the autocrat was all unused to hear. In turn he was detested by the monarch. As negotiator for the spendthrift Prince Ludwig, he was already obnoxious enough; and it sometimes happened that, by way of variety to the customary torrent of invective, the king, after keeping the secretary for hours in his antechamber, would receive him only to turn him rudely out of the room, without hearing a word he had to say."

At last Karl Maria's indignation burst over bounds at some unusual indignity; and he played a practical joke on the king. Meeting an old woman in the palace one day near the door of the royal sanctum, she asked him where she could find the court-washerwoman. "There," said the reckless Weber, pointing to the door of the king's cabinet. The king, who hated old women, was in a transport of rage, and, on her terror-stricken explanation of the intrusion, had no difficulty in fixing the mischief in the right quarter. Weber was thrown into prison, and had it not been for Prince Ludwig's intercession he would have remained there for several years. While confined he managed to compose one of his most beautiful songs, "Ein steter Kampf ist unser Leben." He had not long been released when he was again imprisoned on account of some of his father's wretched follies, that arrogant old gentleman being utterly reckless how he involved others, so long as he carried out his own selfish purposes and indulgence. His friend Danzi, director of the royal opera at Stuttgart, proved his good genius in this instance; for he wrangled with the king till his young friend was released.

Weber's only consolations during this dismal life in Stuttgart were the friendship of Danzi, and his love for a beautiful singer named Gretchen. Danzi was a true mentor and a devoted friend. He was wont to say to Karl: "To be a true artist, you must be a true man." But the lovely Gretchen, however she may have consoled his somewhat arid life, was not a beneficial influence, for she led him into many sad extravagances and an unwholesome taste for playing the cavalier.

In spite of his discouraging surroundings, Weber's creative power was active during this period, and showed how, perhaps unconsciously to himself, he was growing in power and depth of experience. He wrote the cantata "Der erste Ton," a large number of songs, the first of his great piano sonatas, several overtures and symphonies, and the opera "Sylvana" ("Das Waldmädchen" rewritten and enlarged), which, both in its music and libretto, seems to have been the precursor of his great works "Der Freischutz" and "Euryanthe." At the first performance of "Sylvana" in Frankfort, September 16, 1810, he met Miss Caroline Brandt, who sang the principal character. She afterward became his wife, and her love and devotion were the solace of his life.

Weber spent most of the year 1810 in Darmstadt, where he again met Vogler and Meyerbeer. Vogler's severe artistic instructions were of great value to Weber in curbing his extravagance, and impressing on him that restraint was one of the most valuable factors in art. What Vogler thought of Weber we learn from a letter in which he writes: "Had I been forced to leave the world before I found these two, Weber and Meyerbeer, I should have died a miserable man."

III.

It was about this time, while visiting Mannheim, that the idea of "Der Freischutz" first entered his mind. His friend the poet Kind was with him, and they were ransacking an old book, Apel's "Ghost Stories." One of these dealt with the ancient legend of the hunter Bartusch, a woodland myth ranking high in German folk-lore. They were both delighted with the fantastic and striking story, full of the warm coloring of Nature, and the balmy atmosphere of the forest and mountain. They immediately arranged the framework of the libretto, afterward written by Kind, and set to such weird and enchanting music by Weber.

In 1811 Weber began to give concerts, for his reputation was becoming known far and wide as a brilliant composer and virtuoso. For two years he played a round of concerts in Munich, Leipsic, Gotha, Weimar, Berlin, and other places. He was everywhere warmly welcomed. Lichten-stein, in his "Memoir of Weber," writes of his Berlin reception: "Young artists fell on their knees before him; others embraced him wherever they could get at him. All crowded around him, till his head was crowned, not with a chaplet of flowers, but a circlet of happy faces." The devotion of his friends, his happy family relations, the success of his published works, conspired to make Weber cheerful and joyous beyond his wont, for he was naturally of a melancholy and serious turn, disposed to look at life from its tragic side.

In 1813 he was called to Prague to direct the music of the German opera in that Bohemian capital. The Bohemians had always been a highly musical race, and their chief city is associated in the minds of the students of music as the place where many of the great operas were first presented to the public. Mozart loved Prague, for he found in its people the audiences who appreciated and honored him the most. Its traditions were honored in their treatment of Weber, for his three years there were among the happiest of his life.

Our composer wrote his opera of "Der Freischütz" in Dresden. It was first produced in the opera-house of that classic city, but it was not till 1821, when it was performed in Berlin, that its greatness was recognized. Weber can best tell the story of its reception himself. In his letter to his co-author, Kind, he writes:

"The free-shooter has hit the mark. The second representation has succeeded as well as the first; there was the same enthusiasm. All the places in the house are taken for the third, which comes off to-morrow. It is the greatest triumph one can have. You cannot imagine what a lively interest your text inspires from beginning to end. How happy I should have been if you had only been present to hear it for yourself! Some of the scenes produced an effect which I was far from anticipating; for example, that of the young girls. If I see you again at Dresden, I will tell you all about it; for I cannot do it justice in writing. How much I am indebted to you for your magnificent poem! I embrace you with the sincerest emotion, returning to your muse the laurels I owe her. God grant that you may be happy. Love him who loves you with infinite respect. "Your Weber."

"Der Freischütz" was such a success as to place the composer in the front ranks of the lyric stage. The striking originality, the fire, the passion of his music, the ardent national feeling, and the freshness of treatment, gave a genuine shock of delight and surprise to the German world.

IV.

The opera of "Preciosa," also a masterpiece, was given shortly after with great *eclat*, though it failed to inspire the deep enthusiasm which greeted "Der Freischütz." In 1823, "Euryanthe" was produced in Berlin—a work on which Weber exhausted all the treasures of his musical genius. Without the elements of popular success which made his first great opera such an immediate favorite, it shows the most finished and scholarly work which Weber ever attained. Its symmetry and completeness, the elaboration of all the forms, the richness and variety of the orchestration, bear witness to the long and thoughtful labor expended on it. It gradually won its way to popular recognition, and has always remained one of the favorite works of the German stage.

The opera of "Oberon" was Weber's last great production. The celebrated poet Wieland composed the poem underlying the libretto, from the mediæval romance of Huon of Bordeaux. The scenes are laid in fairy-land, and it may be almost called a German "Midsummer-Night's Dream," though the story differs widely from the charming phantasy of our own Shakespeare. The opera of "Oberon" was written for Kemble, of the Covent Garden theatre, in London, and was produced by Weber under circumstances of failing health and great mental depression. The composer pressed every energy to the utmost to meet his engagement, and it was feared by his friends that he would not live to see it put on the stage. It did, indeed, prove the song of the dying swan, for he only lived four months after reaching London. "Oberon" was performed with immense success under the direction of Sir George Smart, and the fading days of the author were cheered by the acclamations of the English public; but the work cost him his life. He died in London, June 5,1826. His last words were: "God reward you for all your kindness to me.—Now let me sleep."

Apart from his dramatic compositions, Weber is known for his many beautiful overtures and symphonies for the orchestra, and his various works for the piano, from sonatas to waltzes and minuets. Among his most pleasing piano-works are the "Invitation to the Waltz," the "Perpetual Rondo," and the "Polonaise in E major." Many of his songs rank among the finest German lyrics. He would have been recognized as an able composer had he not produced great operas; but the superior excellence of these cast all his other compositions in the shade.

Weber was fortunate in having gifted poets to write his dramas. As rich as he was in melodic affluence, his creative faculty seems to have had its tap-root in deep personal feelings and enthusiasms. One of the most poetic and picturesque of composers, he needed a powerful exterior suggestion to give his genius wings and fire. The Germany of his time was alive with patriotic ardor, and the existence of the nation gathered from its emergencies new strength and force. The heart of Weber beat strong with the popular life. Romantic and serious in his taste, his imagination fed on old German tradition and song, and drew from them its richest food. The whole life of the Fatherland, with its glow of love for home, its keen sympathies with the influences of Nature, its fantastic play of thought, its tendency to embody the primitive forces in weird myths, found in Weber an eloquent exponent; and we perceive in his music all the color and vividness of these influences.

Weber's love of Nature was singularly keen. The woods, the mountains, the lakes, and the streams, spoke to his soul with voices full of meaning. He excelled in making these voices speak and sing; and he may, therefore, be entitled the father of the romantic and descriptive school in German operatic music. With more breadth and robustness, he expressed the national feelings of his people, even as Chopin did those of dying Poland. Weber's motives are generally caught from the immemorial airs which resound in every village and hamlet, and the fresh beat of the German heart sends its thrill through almost every bar of his music. Here is found the ultimate significance of his art-work, apart from the mere musical beauty of his compositions.

MENDELSSOHN.

I.

Few careers could present more startling contrasts than those of Mozart and Mendelssohn, in many respects of similar genius, but utterly opposed in the whole surroundings of their lives. Felix Mendelssohn-Bartholdy was the grandson of the celebrated philosopher Moses Mendelssohn, and the son of a rich Hamburg banker. His uncles were distinguished in literary and social life. His friends from early childhood were eminent scholars, poets, painters, and musicians, and his family moved in the most refined and wealthy circles. He was nursed in the lap of luxury, and never knew the cold and hunger of life. All the good fairies and graces seemed to have smiled benignly on his birth, and to have showered on him their richest gifts. Many successful wooers of the muse have been, fortunately for themselves, the heirs of poverty, and became successful only to yield themselves to fat and slothful ease. But, with every incitement to an idle and contented life, Mendelssohn toiled like a galley-slave, and saw in his wealth only the means of a more exclusive consecration to his art. A passionate impulse to labor was the law of his life.

Many will recollect the brilliant novel "Charles Auchester," in which, under the names of Seraphael, Aronach, Charles Auchester, Julia Bennett, and Starwood Burney, are painted the characters of Mendelssohn, Zelter his teacher, Joachim the violinist, Jenny Lind, and Sterndale Bennett the English composer. The brilliant coloring does not disguise nor flatter the lofty Christian purity, the splendid genius, and the great personal charm of the composer, who shares in largest measure the homage which the English public lays at the feet of Handel.

As child and youth Mendelssohn, born at Hamburg, February 3, 1809, displayed the same precocity of talent as was shown by Mozart. Sir Julius Benedict relates his first meeting with him. He was walking in Berlin with Von Weber, and the latter called his attention to a boy about eleven years old, who, perceiving the author of "Der Freischütz," gave him a hearty greeting. "'Tis Felix Mendelssohn," said Weber, introducing the marvelous boy. Benedict narrates his amazement to find the extraordinary attainments of this beautiful youth, with curling auburn hair, brilliant clear eyes, and lips smiling with innocence and candor. Five minutes after young Mendelssohn had astonished his English friend by his admirable performance of several of his own compositions, he forgot Weber, quartets, and counterpoint, to leap over the garden hedges and climb the trees like a squirrel. When scarcely twenty years old he had composed his octet, three quartets for the piano and strings, two sonatas, two symphonies, his first violin quartet, various operas, many songs, and the immortal overture of "A Midsummer-Night's Dream."

Mendelssohn received an admirable education, was an excellent classicist and linguist, and during a short residence at Dusseldorf showed such talent for painting as to excite much wonder. Before he was twenty he was the friend of Goethe and Herder, who delighted in a genius so rich and symmetrical. Some of Goethe's letters are full of charming expressions of praise and affection, for the aged Jupiter of German literature found in the promise of this young Apollo something of the many-sided power which made himself so remarkable.

II.

The Mendelssohn family had moved to Berlin when Felix was only three years old, and the Berliners always claimed him as their own. Strange to say, the city of his birth did not recognize his talent for many years. At the age of twenty he went to England, and the high breeding, personal beauty, and charming manner of the young musician gave him the *entrée* into the most fastidious and exclusive circles. His first symphony and the "Midsummer-Night's Dream" overture stamped his power with the verdict of a warm enthusiasm; for London, though cold and conservative, is prompt to recognize a superior order of merit.

His travels through Scotland inspired Mendelssohn with sentiments of great admiration. The scenery filled his mind with the highest suggestions of beauty and grandeur. He afterward tells us that "he preferred the cold sky and the pines of the north to charming scenes in the midst of landscapes bathed in the glowing rays of the sun and azure light." The vague Ossianic figures that raised their gigantic heads in the fog-wreaths of clouded mountain-tops and lonely lochs had a peculiar fascination for him, and acted like wine on his imagination. The "Hebrides" overture was the fruit of this tour, one of the most powerful and characteristic of his minor compositions. His sister Fanny (Mrs. Hensel) asked him to describe the gray scenery of the north, and he replied in music by improvising his impressions. This theme was afterward worked out in the elaborate overture.

We will not follow him in his various travels through France and Italy. Suffice it to say that his keen and passionate mind absorbed everything in art which could feed the divine hunger, for he was ever discontented, and had his mind fixed on an absolute and determined ideal. During this time of travel he became intimate with the sculptor Thorwaldsen, and the painters Leopold Robert and Horace Vernet. This period produced "Walpurgis Night," the first of the "Songs without Words," the great symphony in A major, and the "Melusine" overture. He is now about to enter on the epoch which puts to the fullest test the varied resources of his genius. To Moscheles he writes, in answer to his old teacher's warm praise: "Your praise is better than three orders of nobility." For several years we see him busy in multifarious ways, composing, leading musical festivals, concert-giving, directing opera-houses, and yet finding time to keep up a busy correspondence with the most distinguished men in Europe; for Mendelssohn seemed to find in letter-writing a rest for his overtaxed brain.

In 1835 he completed his great oratorio of "St. Paul," for Leipsic. The next year he received the title of Doctor of Philosophy and the Fine Arts; and in 1837 he married the charming Cécile Jean-renaud, who made his domestic life so gentle and harmonious. It has been thought strange that Mendelssohn should have made so little mention of his lovely wife in his letters, so prone as he was to speak of affairs of his daily life. Be this as it may, his correspondence with Moscheles, Devrient, and others, as well as the general testimony of his friends, shows us unmistakably that his home-life was blessed in an exceptional degree with intellectual sympathy, and the tenderest, most thoughtful love.

In 1841 Mendelssohn became Kapellmeister of the Prussian court. He now wrote the "Athalie" music, the "Midsummer-Night's Dream," and a large number of lesser pieces, including the "Songs without Words," and piano sonatas, as well as much church music. The greatest work of this period was the "Hymn of Praise," a symphonic cantata for the Leipsic anniversary of the invention of printing, regarded by many as his finest composition.

Mendelssohn always loved England, and made frequent visits across the Channel; for he felt that among the English he was fully appreciated, both as man and composer.

His oratorio of "Elijah" was composed for the English public, and produced at the great Birmingham festival in 1846, under his own direction, with magnificent success. It was given a second time in April, 1847, with his final refinements and revisions; and the event was regarded in England as one of the greatest since the days of Handel, to whom, as well as to Haydn and Beethoven, Mendelssohn showed himself a worthy rival in the field of oratorio composition. Of this visit to England Lampadius, his friend and biographer, writes: "Her Majesty, who as well as her husband was a great friend of art, and herself a distinguished musician, received the distinguished German in her own sitting-room, Prince Albert being the only one present besides herself. As he entered she asked his pardon for the somewhat disorderly state of the room, and began to rearrange the articles with her own hands, Mendelssohn himself gallantly offering his assistance. Some parrots whose cages hung in the room she herself carried into the next room, in which Mendelssohn helped her also. She then requested her guest to play something, and afterward sang some songs of his which she had sung at a court concert soon after the attack on her person. She was not wholly pleased, however, with her own performance, and said pleasantly to Mendelssohn: 'I can do better—ask Lablache if I cannot; but I am afraid of you!'"

This anecdote was related by Mendelssohn himself to show the graciousness of the English queen. It was at this time that Prince Albert sent to Mendelssohn the book of the oratorio "Elijah" with which he used to follow the performance, with the following autographic inscription:

"To the noble artist, who, surrounded by the Baal worship of corrupted art, has been able by his genius and science to preserve faithfully like another Elijah the worship of true art, and once more to accustom our ear, lost in the whirl of an empty play of sounds, to the pure notes of expressive composition and legitimate harmony—to the great master, who makes us conscious of the unity of his conception through the whole maze of his creation, from the soft whispering to the mighty raging of the elements: Written in token of grateful remembrance by Albert. "Buckingham Palace, April 24, 1847."

An occurrence at the Birmingham festival throws a clear light on Mendelssohn's presence of mind, and on his faculty of instant concentration. On the last day, among other things, one of Handel's anthems was given. The concert was already going on, when it was discovered that the short recitative which precedes the "Coronation Hymn," and which the public had in the printed text, was lacking in the voice parts. The directors were perplexed. Mendelssohn, who was sitting in an ante-room of the hall, heard of it, and said, "Wait, I will help you." He sat down directly at a table, and composed the music for the recitative and the orchestral accompaniment in about half an hour. It was at once transcribed, and given without any rehearsal, and went very finely.

On returning to Leipsic he determined to pass the summer in Vevay, Switzerland, on account of his failing health, which had begun to alarm himself and his friends. His letters from Switzerland at this period show how the shadow of rapidly approaching death already threw a deep gloom over his habitually cheerful nature. He returned to Leipsic, and resumed hard work. His operetta entitled "Return from among Strangers" was his last production, with the exception of some lively songs and a few piano pieces of the "Lieder ohne Worte," or "Songs without Words," series. Mendelssohn was seized with an apoplectic attack on October 9, 1847. Second and third seizures quickly followed, and he died November 4th, aged thirty-eight years.

All Germany and Europe sorrowed over the loss of this great musician, and his funeral was attended by many of the most distinguished persons from all parts of the land, for the loss was felt to be something like a national calamity.

III.

Mendelssohn was one of the most intelligent and scholarly composers of the century. Learned in various branches of knowledge, and personally a man of unusual accomplishments, his career was full of manly energy, enlightened enthusiasm, and severe devotion to the highest forms of the art of music. Not only his great oratorios, "St. Paul" and "Elijah," but his music for the piano, including the "Songs without Words," sonatas, and many occasional pieces, have won him a high place among his musical brethren. As an orchestral composer, his overtures are filled with strikingly original thoughts and elevated conceptions, expressed with much delicacy of instrumental coloring. He was brought but little in contact with the French and Italian schools, and there is found in his works a severity of art-form which shows how closely he sympathized with Bach and Handel in his musical tendencies. He died while at the very zenith of his powers, and we may well believe that a longer life would have developed much richer beauty in his compositions. Short as his career was, however, he left a great number of magnificent works, which entitle him to a place among the Titans of music.

RICHARD WAGNER.
I.

It is curious to note how often art-controversy has become edged with a bitterness rivaling even the gall and venom of religious dispute. Scholars have not yet forgotten the fiery war of words which raged between Richard Bentley and his opponents concerning the authenticity of the "Epistles of Phalaris," nor how literary Germany was divided into two hostile camps by Wolf's attack on the personality of Homer. It is no less fresh in the minds of critics how that modern Jupiter, Lessing, waged a long and bitter battle with the Titans of the French classical drama, and finally crushed them with the thunderbolt of the "Dramaturgie;" nor what acrimony sharpened the discussion between the rival theorists in music, Gluck and Piccini, at Paris. All of the intensity of these art-campaigns, and many of the conditions of the last, enter into the contest between Richard Wagner and the *Italianissimi* of the present day.

The exact points at issue were for a long time so befogged by the smoke of the battle that many of the large class who are musically interested, but never had an opportunity to study the question, will find an advantage in a clear and comprehensive sketch of the facts and principles involved. Until recently, there were still many people who thought of Wagner as a youthful and eccentric enthusiast, all afire with misdirected genius, a mere carpet-knight on the sublime battle-field of art, a beginner just sowing his wild-oats in works like "Lohengrin," "Tristan and Iseult," or the "Rheingold." It is a revelation full of suggestive value for these to realize that he is a musical thinker, ripe with sixty years of labor and experience; that he represents the rarest and choicest fruits of modern culture, not only as musician, but as poet and philosopher; that he is one of the few examples in the history of the art where massive scholarship and the power of subtle analysis have been united, in a preeminent degree, with great creative genius. Preliminary to a study of what Wagner and his disciples entitle the "Artwork of the Future," let us take a swift survey of music as a medium of expression for the beautiful, and some of the forms which it has assumed.

This Ariel of the fine arts sends its messages to the human soul by virtue of a fourfold capacity: Firstly, the imitation of the voices of Nature, such as the winds, the waves, and the cries of animals; secondly, its potential delight as melody, modulation, rhythm, harmony—in other words, its simple worth as a "thing of beauty," without regard to cause or consequence; thirdly, its force of boundless suggestion; fourthly, that affinity for union with the more definite and exact forms of the imagination (poetry), by which the intellectual context of the latter is raised to a far higher power of grace, beauty, passion, sweetness, without losing individuality of outline—like, indeed, the hazy aureole which painters set on the brow of the man Jesus, to fix the seal of the ultimate Divinity. Though several or all of these may be united in the same composition, each musical work may be characterized in the main as descriptive, sensuous, suggestive, or dramatic, according as either element contributes most largely to its purpose. Simple melody or harmony appeals mostly to the sensuous love of sweet sounds. The symphony does this in an enlarged and complicated sense, but is still more marked by the marvelous suggestive energy with which it unlocks all the secret raptures of fancy, floods the border-lands of thought with a glory not to be found on sea or land, and paints ravishing pictures, that come and go like dreams, with colors drawn from the "twelve-tinted tone-spectrum."

Shelley describes this peculiar influence of music in his "Prometheus Unbound," with exquisite beauty and truth:

"My soul is an enchanted boat,
Which, like a sleeping swan, doth float
Upon the silver waves of thy sweet singing;
And thine doth like an angel sit
Beside the helm conducting it,
While all the waves with melody are ringing.
It seems to float ever, forever,
Upon that many-winding river,
Between mountains, woods, abysses,
A paradise of wildernesses."

As the symphony best expresses the suggestive potency in music, the operatic form incarnates its capacity of definite thought, and the expression of that thought. The term "lyric," as applied to the genuine operatic conception, is a misnomer. Under the accepted operatic form, however, it has relative truth, as the main musical purpose of opera seems, hitherto, to have been less to furnish expression for exalted emotions and thoughts, or exquisite sentiments, than to grant the vocal *virtuoso* opportunity to display phenomenal qualities of voice and execution. But all opera, however it may stray from the fundamental idea, suggests this dramatic element in music, just as mere lyricism in the poetic art is the blossom from which is unfolded the full-blown perfection of the word-drama, the highest form of all poetry.

II.

That music, by and of itself, cannot express the intellectual element in the beautiful dream-images of art with precision, is a palpable truth. Yet, by its imperial dominion over the sphere of emotion and sentiment, the connection of the latter with complicated mental phenomena is made to bring into the domain of tone vague and shifting fancies and pictures. How much further music can be made to assimilate to the other arts in directness of mental suggestion, by wedding to it the noblest forms of poetry, and making each the complement of the other, is the knotty problem which underlies the great art-controversy about which this article concerns itself. On the one side we have the claim that music is the all-sufficient law unto itself; that its appeal to sympathy is through the intrinsic sweetness of harmony and tune, and the intellect must be satisfied with what it may accidentally glean in this harvest-field; that, in the rapture experienced in the sensuous apperception of its beauty, lies the highest phase of art-sensibility. Therefore, concludes the syllogism, it matters nothing as to the character of the libretto or poem to whose words the music is arranged, so long as the dramatic framework suffices as a support for the flowery festoons of song, which drape its ugliness and beguile attention by the fascinations of bloom and grace. On the other hand, the apostles of the new musical philosophy insist that art is something more than a vehicle for the mere sense of the beautiful, an exquisite provocation wherewith to startle the sense of a selfish, epicurean pleasure; that its highest function—to follow the idea of the Greek Plato, and the greatest of his modern disciples, Schopenhauer—is to serve as the incarnation of the true and the good; and, even as Goethe makes the Earth-Spirit sing in "Faust"—

"'Tis thus over at the loom of Time I ply,
And weave for God the garment thou seest him by"—

so the highest art is that which best embodies the immortal thought of the universe as reflected in the mirror of man's consciousness; that music, as speaking the most spiritual language of any of the art-family, is burdened with the most pressing responsibility as the interpreter between the finite and the infinite; that all its forms must be measured by the earnestness and success with which they teach and suggest what is best in aspiration and truest in thought; that music, when wedded to the highest form of poetry (the drama), produces the consummate art-result, and sacrifices to some extent its power of suggestion, only to acquire a greater glory and influence, that of investing definite intellectual images with spiritual raiment, through which they shine on the supreme altitudes of ideal thought; that to make this marriage perfect as an art-form and fruitful in result, the two partners must come as equals, neither one the drudge of the other; that in this organic fusion music and poetry contribute, each its best, to emancipate art from its thralldom to that which is merely trivial, commonplace, and accidental, and make it a revelation of all that is most exalted in thought, sentiment, and purpose. Such is the aesthetic theory of Richard Wagner's art-work.

III.

It is suggestive to note that the earliest recognized function of music, before it had learned to enslave itself to mere sensuous enjoyment, was similar in spirit to that which its latest reformer demands for it in the art of the future. The glory of its birth then shone on its brow. It was the handmaid and minister of the religious instinct. The imagination became afire with the mystery of life and Nature, and burst into the flames and frenzies of rhythm. Poetry was born, but instantly sought the wings of music for a higher flight than the mere word would permit. Even the great epics of the "Iliad" and "Odyssey" were originally sung or chanted by the Ilomerido, and the same essential union seems to have been in some measure demanded afterward in the Greek drama, which, at its best, was always inspired with the religious sentiment. There is every reason to believe that the chorus of the drama of Æschylus, Sophocles, and Euripides uttered their comments on the action of the play with such a prolongation and variety of pitch in the rhythmic intervals as to constitute a sustained and melodic recitative. Music at this time was an essential part of the drama. When the creative genius of Greece had set toward its ebb, they were divorced, and music was only set to lyric forms. Such remained the status of the art till, in the Italian Renaissance, modern opera was born in the reunion of music and the drama. Like the other arts, it assumed at the outset to be a mere revival of antique traditions. The great poets of Italy had then passed way, and it was left for music to fill the void.

The muse, Polyhymnia, soon emerged from the stage of childish stammering. Guittone di Arezzo taught her to fix her thoughts in indelible signs, and two centuries of training culminated in the inspired composers, Orlando di Lasso and Pales-trina. Of the gradual degradation of the operatic art as its forms became more elaborate and fixed; of the arbitrary transfer of absolute musical forms like the aria, duet, finale, etc., into the action of the opera without regard to poetic propriety; of the growing tendency to treat the human voice like any other instrument, merely to show its resources as an organ; of the final utter bondage of the poet to the musician, till opera became little more than a congeries of musico-gymnastic forms, wherein the vocal soloists could display their art, it needs not to speak at length, for some of these vices have not yet disappeared. In the language of Dante's guide through the Inferno, at one stage of their wanderings, when the sights were peculiarly mournful and desolate—

"Non raggioniam da lor, ma guarda e passa."

The loss of all poetic verity and earnestness in opera furnished the great composer Gluck with the motive of the bitter and protracted contest which he waged with varying success throughout Europe, though principally in Paris. Gluck boldly affirmed, and carried out the principle in his compositions, that the task of dramatic music was to accompany the different phases of emotion in the text, and give them their highest effect of spiritual intensity. The singer must be the mouthpiece of the poet, and must take extreme care in giving the full poetical burden of the song. Thus, the declamatory music became of great importance, and Gluck's recitative reached an unequaled degree of perfection.

The critics of Gluck's time hurled at him the same charges which are familiar to us now as coming from the mouths and pens of the enemies of Wagner's music. Yet Gluck, however conscious of the ideal unity between music and poetry, never thought of bringing this about by a sacrifice of any of the forms of his own peculiar art. His influence, however, was very great, and the traditions of the great *maestro's* art have been kept alive in the works of his no less great disciples, Méhul, Cherubini, Spontini, and Meyerbeer.

Two other attempts to ingraft new and vital power on the rigid and trivial sentimentality of the Italian forms of opera were those of Rossini and Weber. The former was gifted with the greatest affluence of pure melodiousness ever given to a composer. But even his sparkling originality and freshness did little more than reproduce the old forms under a more attractive guise. Weber, on the other hand, stood in the van of a movement which had its fountain-head in the strong romantic and national feeling, pervading the whole of society and literature. There was a general revival of mediaeval and popular poetry, with its balmy odor of the woods, and fields, and streams. Weber's melody was the direct offspring of the tunefulness of the German *Volkslied*, and so it expressed, with wonderful freshness and beauty, all the range of passion and sentiment within the limits of this pure and simple language. But the boundaries were far too narrow to build upon them the ultimate union of music and poetry, which should express the perfect harmony of the two arts. While it is true that all of the great German composers protested, by their works, against the spirit and character of the Italian school of music, Wagner claims that the first abrupt and strongly-defined departure toward a radical reform in art is found in Beethoven's Ninth Symphony with chorus. Speaking of this remarkable leap from instrumental to vocal music in a professedly symphonic composition, Wagner, in his "Essay on Beethoven," says: "We declare that the work of art, which was formed and quickened entirely by that deed, must present the most perfect artistic form, i.e., that form in which, as for the drama, so also and especially for music, every conventionality would be abolished." Beethoven is asserted to have founded the new musical school, when he admitted, by his recourse to the vocal cantata in the greatest of his symphonic works, that he no longer recognized absolute music as sufficient unto itself.

In Bach and Handel, the great masters of fugue and counterpoint; in Rossini, Mozart, and Weber, the consummate creators of melody—then, according to this view, we only recognize thinkers in the realm of pure music. In Beethoven, the greatest of them all, was laid the basis of the new epoch of tone-poetry. In the immortal songs of Schubert, Schumann, Mendelssohn, Liszt, and Franz, and the symphonies of the first four, the vitality of the reformatory idea is richly illustrated. In the music-drama of Wagner, it is claimed by his disciples, is found the full flower and development of the art-work.

William Richard Wagner, the formal projector of the great changes whose details are yet to be sketched, was born at Leipsic in 1813. As a child he displayed no very marked artistic tastes, though his ear and memory for music were quite remarkable. When admitted to the Kreuzschule of Dresden, the young student, however, distinguished himself by his very great talent for literary composition and the classical languages. To this early culture, perhaps, we are indebted for the great poetic power which has enabled him to compose the remarkable libretti which have furnished the basis of his music. His first creative attempt was a blood-thirsty drama, where forty-two characters are killed, and the few survivors are haunted by the ghosts. Young Wagner soon devoted himself to the study of music, and, in 1833, became a pupil of Theodor Weinlig, a distinguished teacher of harmony and counterpoint. His four years of study at this time were also years of activity in creative experiment, as he composed four operas.

His first opera of note was "Rienzi," with which he went to Paris in 1837. In spite of Meyerbeer's efforts in its favor, this work was rejected, and laid aside for some years. Wagner supported himself by musical criticism and other literary work, and soon was in a position to offer another opera, "Der fliegende Holländer," to the authorities of the Grand Opera-House. Again the directors refused the work, but were so charmed with the beauty of the libretto that they bought it to be reset to music. Until the year 1842, life was a trying struggle for the indomitable young musician. "Rienzi" was then produced at Dresden, so much to the delight of the King of Saxony that the composer was made royal Kapellmeister and leader of the orchestra. The production of "Der fliegende Holländer" quickly followed; next came "Tanhäuser" and "Lohengrin," to be swiftly succeeded by the "Meistersinger von Nürnberg." This period of our *maestro's* musical activity also commenced to witness the development of his theories on the philosophy of his art, and some of his most remarkable critical writings were then given to the world.

Political troubles obliged Wagner to spend seven years of exile in Zurich; thence he went to London, where he remained till 1861 as conductor of the London Philharmonic Society. In 1861 the exile returned to his native country, and spent several years in Germany and Russia—there having arisen quite a *furore* for his music in the latter country. The enthusiasm awakened in the breast of King Louis of Bavaria by "Der fliegende Holländer" resulted in a summons to Wagner to settle at Munich, and with the glories of the Royal Opera-House in that city his name has since been principally connected. The culminating art-splendor of his life, however, was the production of his stupendous tetralogy, the "Ring der Nibelungen," at the great opera-house at Baireuth, in the summer of the year 1876.

IV.

The first element to be noted in Wagner's operatic forms is the energetic protest against the artificial and conventional in music. The utter want of dramatic symmetry and fitness in the operas we have been accustomed to hear could only be overlooked by the force of habit, and the tendency to submerge all else in the mere enjoyment of the music. The utter variance of music and poetry was to Wagner the stumbling-block which, first of all, must be removed. So he crushed at one stroke all the hard, arid forms which existed in the lyrical drama as it had been known. His opera, then, is no longer a congeries of separate musical numbers, like duets, arias, chorals, and finales, set in a flimsy web of formless recitative, without reference to dramatic economy. His great purpose is lofty dramatic truth, and to this end he sacrifices the whole framework of accepted musical forms, with the exception of the chorus, and this he remodels. The musical energy is concentrated in the dialogue as the main factor of the dramatic problem, and fashioned entirely according to the requirements of the action. The continuous flow of beautiful melody takes the place alike of the dry recitative and the set musical forms which characterize the accepted school of opera. As the dramatic *motif* demands, this "continuous melody" rises into the highest ecstasies of the lyrical fervor, or ebbs into a chant-like swell of subdued feeling, like the ocean after the rush of the storm. If Wagner has destroyed musical forms, he has also added a positive element. In place of the aria we have the *logos*. This is the musical expression of the principal passion underlying the action of the drama. Whenever, in the course of the development of the story, this passion comes into ascendency, the rich strains of the *logos* are heard anew, stilling all other sounds. Gounod has, in part, applied this principle in "Faust." All opera-goers will remember the intense dramatic effect arising from the recurrence of the same exquisite lyric outburst from the lips of Marguerite.

The peculiar character of Wagner's word-drama next arouses critical interest and attention. The composer is his own poet, and his creative genius shines no less here than in the world of tone. The musical energy flows entirely from the dramatic conditions, like the electrical current from the cups of the battery; and the rhythmical structure of the *melos* (tune) is simply the transfiguration of the poetical basis. The poetry, then, is all-important in the music-drama. Wagner has rejected the forms of blank verse and rhyme as utterly unsuited to the lofty purposes of music, and has gone to the metrical principle of all the Teutonic and Slavonic poetry. This rhythmic element of alliteration, or *staffrhyme*, we find magnificently illustrated in the Scandinavian Eddas, and even in our own Anglo-Saxon fragments of the days of Cædmon and Alcuin. By the use of this new form, verse and melody glide together in one exquisite rhythm, in which it seems impossible to separate the one from the other. The strong accents of the alliterating syllables supply the music with firmness, while the low-toned syllables give opportunity for the most varied *nuances* of declamation.

The first radical development of Wagner's theories we see in "The Flying Dutchman." In "Tanhhäser" and "Lohengrin" they find full sway. The utter revolt of his mind from the trivial and commonplace sentimentalities of Italian opera led him to believe that the most heroic and lofty motives alone should furnish the dramatic foundation of opera. For a while he oscillated between history and legend, as best adapted to furnish his material. In his selection of the dream-land of myth and legend, we may detect another example of the profound and *exigeant* art-instincts which have ruled the whole of Wagner's life. There could be no question as to the utter incongruity of any dramatic picture of ordinary events, or ordinary personages, finding expression in musical utterance. Genuine and profound art must always be consistent with itself, and what we recognize as general truth. Even characters set in the comparatively near back-ground of history are too closely related to our own familiar surroundings of thought and mood to be regarded as artistically natural in the use of music as the organ of the every-day life of emotion and sentiment. But with the dim and heroic shapes that haunt the border-land of the supernatural, which we call legend, the case is far different. This is the drama of the demigods, living in a different atmosphere from our own, however akin to ours may be their passions and purposes. For these we are no longer compelled to regard the medium of music as a forced and untruthful expression, for do they not dwell in the magic lands of the imagination? All sense of dramatic inconsistency instantly vanishes, and the conditions of artistic illusion are perfect.

"'Tis distance lends enchantment to the view,

And clothes the mountains with their azure hue."

Thus all of Wagner's works, from "Der fliegende Hollander" to the "Ring der Nibelungen," have been located in the world of myth, in obedience to a profound art-principle. The opera of "Tristan and Iseult," first performed in 1865, announced Wagner's absolute emancipation, both in the construction of music and poetry, from the time-honored and time-corrupted canons, and, aside from the last great work, it may be received as the most perfect representation of his school.

The third main feature in the Wagner music is the wonderful use of the orchestra as a factor in the solution of the art-problem. This is no longer a mere accompaniment to the singer, but translates the passion of the play into a grand symphony, running parallel and commingling with the vocal music. Wagner, as a great master of orchestration, has had few equals since Beethoven; and he uses his power with marked effect to heighten the dramatic intensity of the action, and at the same time to convey certain meanings which can only find vent in the vague and indistinct forms of pure music. The romantic conception of the mediæval love, the shudderings and raptures of Christian revelation, have certain phases that absolute music alone can express. The orchestra, then, becomes as much an integral part of the music-drama, in its actual current movement, as the chorus or the leading performers. Placed on the stage, yet out of sight, its strains might almost be fancied the sound of the sympathetic communion of good and evil spirits, with whose presence mystics formerly claimed man was constantly surrounded. Wagner's use of the orchestra may be illustrated from the opera of "Lohengrin."

The ideal background, from which the emotions of the human actors in the drama are reflected with supernatural light, is the conception of the "Holy Graal," the mystic symbol of the Christian faith, and its descent from the skies, guarded by hosts of seraphim. This is the subject of the orchestral prelude, and never have the sweetnesses and terrors of the Christian ecstasy been more potently expressed. The prelude opens with long-drawn chords of the violins, in the highest octaves, in the most exquisite *pianissimo*. The inner eye of the spirit discerns in this the suggestion of shapeless white clouds, hardly discernible from the aerial blue of the sky. Suddenly the strings seem to sound from the farthest distance, in continued *pianissimo*, and the melody, the Graal-motive, takes shape. Gradually, to the fancy, a group of angels seem to reveal themselves, slowly descending from the heavenly heights, and bearing in their midst the *Sangréal*. The modulations throb through the air, augmenting in richness and sweetness, till the *fortissimo* of the full orchestra reveals the sacred mystery. With this climax of spiritual ecstasy the harmonious waves gradually recede and ebb away in dying sweetness, as the angels return to their heavenly abode. This orchestral movement recurs in the opera, according to the laws of dramatic fitness, and its melody is heard also in the *logos* of Lohengrin, the knight of the Graal, to express certain phases of his action. The immense power which music is thus made to have in dramatic effect can easily be fancied.

A fourth prominent characteristic of the Wagner music-drama is that, to develop its full splendor, there must be a cooperation of all the arts, painting, sculpture, and architecture, as well as poetry and music. Therefore, in realizing its effects, much importance rests in the visible beauties of action, as they may be expressed by the painting of scenery and the grouping of human figures. Well may such a grand conception be called the "Art-work of the Future."

Wagner for a long time despaired of the visible execution of his ideas. At last the celebrated pianist Tausig suggested an appeal to the admirers of the new music throughout the world for means to carry out the composer's great idea, viz., to perform the "Nibelungen" at a theatre to be erected for the purpose, and by a select company, in the manner of a national festival, and before an audience entirely removed from the atmosphere of vulgar theatrical shows. After many delays Wagner's hopes were attained, and in the summer of 1876 a gathering of the principal celebrities of Europe was present to criticise the fully perfected fruit of the composer's theories and genius. This festival was so recent, and its events have been the subject of such elaborate comment, that further description will be out of place here.

As a great musical poet, rather epic than dramatic in his powers, there can be no question as to Wagner's rank. The performance of the "Nibelungenring," covering "Rheingold," "Die Walküren," "Siegfried," and "Götterdämmerung," was one of the epochs of musical Germany. However deficient Wagner's skill in writing for the human voice, the power and symmetry of his conceptions, and his genius in embodying them in massive operatic forms, are such as to storm even the prejudices of his opponents. The poet-musician rightfully claims that in his music-drama is found that wedding of two of the noblest of the arts, pregnantly suggested by Shakespeare:

"If Music and sweet Poetry both agree,
As they must needs, the sister and the brother;
One God is God of both, as poets feign."

THE END.

Printed in Great Britain
by Amazon